Red Rose Petals
—
A Poetry Collection

Dana Djokic

Copyright © 2006, 2008 by Dana Djokic

All rights reserved, including the right of
reproduction in whole or in part
in any form.

ISBN 978-0-6151-9768-5

Cover Photo –
Red Rose by Irina Tischenko
(www.bigstockphoto.com)

Self-published
with the assistance of
www.Lulu.com

Printed in the United States of America
March 2008

To Mileta and Diana,
my most perfect roses.

—

Dana Djokic

To Write A Poem

To write a poem
Is like breathing fresh air -
I write about what I care

To write a poem
Is like shaking off emotion -
I write to fulfill my devotion

To write a poem
Is like loving and living -
I write because there's nothing like giving
A part of myself.

1980s' Design

As I walk along, I see the Glamour
Shining out through the street
She walks along with her cotton chiffon
Pressed and printed neat
Across the cobbles, filled with flair
Aqua and pink statues in their hair
The spark of stripes across their skin
Polyester is out and leather is in
White lace is sweet and velvet is bright
But too old and cheap is never right
Off the shoulder and above the knee
She shines above the vivid crowd
Red, yellow, turquoise and green tea
Vulnerable is soft and exhilaration is loud
The gold, the steel, the greasy spike
Behind the ear or in the air
A symbol of self and no animosity or dislike
The neck will shimmer, the head will be tied
The waist is slim, any more is denied
The glance is darkened by a black streak
Thunder is amidst this distinct sight
The pattern of suede is so unique
The black of the face should never be light
Put forth the designer whose art is wicked
The switch goes on and the music can kick it:
    The Cats go Stray and Slim is Jim
    The Men are At Work in a Land Down Under
    The rhythm is Euro, along with Sweet Dreams
    Boy George is pretty, and I wonder
    Captain Sensible said What?
    Bananarama isn't shy
    The Clash is calling
    Eat a Cannibal and sigh--
She closes the glass and stops at the window
The manikin smiles with her false fame
She sits by her board with a palette of colors
The design is so perfect along with her name.

My Style

My style is my own
Nobody will change it
No, it's not a gimmick
It's I, and I alone

My style is my love
Just try to derange it
No, it's not a put-on
It's an image from above

My style, I created
No one can copy it
No, it's not simple
It's mind and soul-related

My style is my obsession
They just can't imagine
Yes, it's eternal
It's my deceptive profession.

Talk; Just Talk

In Our House, there will always be Madness,
U2 can start a war;
We have so many Altered Images,
It's a mistake to accept more.

Just when you think of Fascination,
WHAM! another Bad Boy;
Always Wishing for a Flock of Seagulls,
To find Boy, Jon, Mikey and Roy.

The Human League is always changing
Duran Duran has something I should know.
It IS a nice day for a White Wedding,
But YAZ doesn't want you to go.

If punk's best friend is Bow Wow Wow,
Then it will soon be true;
We will all become faithful ants,
And the Mexicans won't get over
The Wall of VooDoo.

You're Just a Punk

You're just a punk
With your walk and your talk
You have no direction
Your mind's full of junk

You're tough with your leather
And strong with your chain
You live on destruction
And your mind feels no pain

Just tell me, you punk
Why can't you be you?
Get rid of all that black
And that ugly tattoo

You won't live forever
So go on and do what you do
When the day comes
Your image will die too.

If Anyone Asks

Your hair is green
Your jewelry is junk
If anyone asks
You're into punk

Your pride is leather
You don't dance -- you slam
If anyone asks,
You know how to jam

If anyone asks
You don't have a cure
The answer is punk
And that's for sure!

Time

Time,
Oh what a precious thing
It carries my life
On its sturdy wings

I can follow my dreams with time
It helps me along
With visions of hope and success
It helps me be strong

My strength is not enough for me
Time helps it improve
My failures are natural
Which time will remove

Time,
It's made me into what I am
Just perfect for me.

He's The One I Love

He's like all the rest
Doesn't care
Thinks he's the best
Acts like I'm not there

I don't need him at all
He's made me cry
He's let me fall
And won't explain why

He's got a childish mind
And won't play fair
He's not my kind
His talk is air

He'll never understand
He thinks he's so above
What can I do?
When he's the one I love.

They'll Always Be The Same

Some people never seem to change
They are always the same
Day after day, year after year
It's really a shame

The globe is always spinning
And the time can't stand still
So why don't people change
At their own free will?

Their moods are different
As they grow and mature
But why do their images
Always seem so obscure?

So many styles to be found all around
So many ways to be expressed
Why should people go on being normal
In the ways they are dressed?

Some people just won't change
No matter what you do
They'll always be the same
They'll never try anything new.

When The Color Changes

When the color changes
I'm standing all alone
Looking for retreat
A place that's my own

It lasts for a moment
And captures my fear
I can't let it escape
It will soon disappear

When the color changes
The soul is faint
There is no distinction
But the image is quaint

An illusion of feelings
All built up inside
The sensation of space
In which to confide

When the color changes
The mood is banned
And no one emerges
To offer a hand

The colors are mixed
My understanding will lack
Of the cruel misgivings
Which turn everything black.

When It Rains, I Think Of You

The sky is green
The trees are blue
And when it rains
I think of you

Like thundering waves
You live in my mind
Portraying an obsession
Of a different kind

The fallen red leaves
Have all floated away
I've sat here and watched
It rain all day

Sooner or later
The sun will come out
Old leaves will be replaced by new
But when it rains
The thunder is faint
And still, I think of you.

If You Don't Approve

Although it's not your place to say
How you feel about the way I am
You go and say it anyway
As though I'm supposed to understand

At times you make me feel so low
By those smirks you try to hide
I wonder if you really know
How it makes me feel inside

I try to take it all I can
Without seeming to be rude
But there you go with another plan
To totally deflate my mood

Though you'll never change how you are
And I don't want to waste my time
I'll make it without your comments by far
So if you don't approve, it's your own crime.

This Reminds Me

This reminds me of a day
A day we left so far behind
A beautiful, sunny day
That lingers in my mind

This reminds me of the day
When happiness was so bright
We needed nothing more
Than to live our lives right

This reminds me of that day
Which set free all desires
To be a part of love and life
As it so soon expires

There will come another day
Which will be just as fine
As that day I've always wanted
But never could make mine.

The Rhythm

The rhythm takes me for a ride
Beyond the normal feeling of living
It picks me up with a natural high
And never stops giving

From fast, then slow, to moderately mellow
It keeps me feeling how I should
The fun of the beat and glow of the lights
Make me feel so very good

The rhythm of music rotates the world
It changes with time and age
Remember, it never loses its rhythm
But becomes another well-kept page

The rhythm gives a lift to my heart
When I need to shake off the blues
It picks up where depression left off
Leaving me with no dues.

This Time

This time could be the right time
What I've waited for so long
It has been a long hard climb
And all my decisions haven't proved wrong

This time I've reached where I want to be
It's fine and sunny and very nice
I've worked all my life just to be free
And I've done it on my own advice

This time is surely the right time
And with pride and esteem I shall say
My time has finally reached its prime
And I'll take it from here my own way.

When Lightning Strikes

When lightning strikes
I lift my head to see
Without fair warning
It strikes me

The sharpest of lightning
Much sharper than knives
Portrays no mercy
On mine of all lives

Why hast thou shown
Thy cruelty of mind
To subdue a spirit
Of this rare kind

The lightning that strikes
Leaves scars of fear
Never to fade
Until the reason is clear.

One Day Will Be Mine

One day will be mine
When the trickling of my tears
Will finally stop on my face
As I'm drained from all my fears

This day will be all mine
To kneel down on the grass
And yell out with all fury
The degradations I've let pass

Yes, this day will be mine
When the earth will tremble and shake
And God will return the evils
That fools incessantly make.

Suddenly

And suddenly
No one was left inside of me
No longer could I fight
The powers of the light
That reached into my soul
And grabbed what was my goal.

Thank You

May I please say thank you,
for looking away
for bringing me down
for making my day
for painting a frown
for cutting me low
for not letting me finish
for making me go
for being so skittish
for leaving me here
for stepping on me
for throwing your spear
for not letting me be
Thank you, and I wish healthy existence
For you, my friend
Who needs assistance
In manner, coordination and judgment
And to have some sort of cool
When you open up your mouth
And label yourself a fool.

Cascades

Tiny drops of crystal
Fall desperately to the floor
Like little cool cascades
Then they aren't there anymore

Like diamonds, they will glitter
And like kittens, they will cry
But my teardrops are just water
That never seem to dry.

Tell Me

Look into my eyes
And tell me what you see
A field full of roses
Waiting for you and me

Take my welcoming hand
And tell me what you feel
A warm and loving touch
That could only be so real

Place your ear next to my heart
And tell me what you hear
The thundering sound of love
That gives us nothing to fear

Now I'll tell you what I think
While we're dancing close together
Wouldn't it be wonderful
To stay like this forever?

Fatal Attraction

It's got to be you
I just know it
I can feel it

Ever since we talked
I've felt so good
So very good

You seemed so interested
You really did
I know you did

I can feel better about life
I really can
I know I can

Now I love you
I really do
I know I do.

Tell Me (2)

Why don't you just tell me
What it is that's wrong with you
And why you act so foolish
At everything I say or do.

To Plant A Garden

I just put my fist
Through a brick wall
I looked at the other side
And wanted to fall

It surged throughout my body
It hit like a ton
I wanted it to be two
But there's still only one

I just jumped through the ground
It was a familiar place
Cold, dark and solitary
No curtains with lovely lace

I just wanted to plant a garden
But the holes were too small for the seeds
I waited and waited for the flowers to grow
But all that came up were weeds.

Some Day Soon

I was searching for something not there
And it has brought me down here
      There was no flair
      There was no spark
      There was no glare

I was searching for an emotion
And developed a mistaken devotion
      There was no hold
      There was no love
      I always felt cold

Some day soon I'll learn to let go
Some day soon everyone will know
      There was no care
      There was no respect
      I should have been aware.

Sing

I'd sing you a love song
If I knew how to sing
I'd offer you my love
If I knew what yours would bring

I'd sweat through fire
If I knew how to dance
I'd make you feel worth it
If you'd give me the chance.

Free to Dream

Free to dream
About silver and gold
About stunning strength
To make us feel bold

Free to dream
About trust and love
Feelings from others
To set us above

Free to dream
About happiness and health
High expectations
That lead us to wealth

It's the dream that wages
The battle against life
But it's the reality brought out
That cuts like a knife.

He Will Yell

At the littlest things
He will yell
And as he does
It feels like Hell

There he goes again
Like a sickly soul
Tearing away
At my innocent goal

I'll never forgive
For the misery and pain
He's caused my life
Because he couldn't abstain

And at his grave
Only a moment I'll stand
Walking away with relief
Toward a more peaceful land.

The Meaning

It's the meaning
Not the screening
That you have to know
Before you show
How you feel
In a world so real

Without the meaning
We'd be leaning
On a lightless pole
In a filthy hole
Dug ever so deep
Where the ground hogs sleep.

Here's a Dime

Here's a dime
For your smile
That I haven't seen
In such a while

Here's a dime
For your inconvenience
That I might have caused
Because of my lenience

Here's a dime
Now take it and scram
If you can't smile
Why should I give a damn?

From Brother to Brother

From brother to brother
Have nerve -- will travel
She doesn't know when to quit
Throw her some gravel!

They're both very handsome
But certainly not the same
With both on her hands
She thinks it's a game

From brother to brother
She'll giggle and drool
But playing with brothers
Is not very cool!

Shout

And on this day
While the sun is out
Plan it your way
Get up and shout

Don't take their word
Unless you want to be used
Don't believe what you've heard
Unless you want to be abused

Be your own man
It's the only way
Have confidence and you can
Today's the perfect day.

Dance

Dance!
Set your body free
Move!
Come on and move with me

Keep your heart
Moving fast and slow
Let your feet skip
Move 'em any way they go

Now give me
What your body's got
Dance!
And let it get real hot

Move!
And don't you dare be slow
'Cause when I start to dance
I'm gonna let it all go.

Moonlight

The moonlight reaches into my room
Pulls me in its arms
Shakes me with its charms

Under the moonlight, while I'm sitting next to you
You hold me by your side
There's no place else I'd rather hide

And when it fades to another world
I'll still be sitting here
With you, my only dear.

1-2-3

I've got one:
The world's in my hand
I feel just grand
Let's have some fun

I've got two:
Let's check out a book
Learn how to cook
And feed animals in the zoo

I've got three:
Let's go buy a boat
Learn how to float
And live in the glorious sea

I've got one:
Been writing a long time
Can't find the right rhyme
And I'm still not done

I've got two:
The world's bigger than I thought
Can't make it alone
I need you.

I'm Here

I'm here
It took so long
But I'm really here
Where I belong

What a relief
I've left them all behind
I've broken away
This time I won't be blind

I'll start out fair
And watch for the cracks
It's goodbye to them
If they turn their backs

But still, I'm here
My eyes open wide
Ready for anyone
Who tries to deny.

It's You

It's you behind the stares
The one who doesn't care
And you better not dare

Try and put one over me
Because you'll see
How Hell can be

It's you behind the doors
Lying even more
Covering from before

You played your silly game
Trying to reach fame
Only lowering your name

It's you
I can see right through
You think I'm blind?
You expect me to be kind?
Give me a break!
I've had all I could take!
Can't hide behind those eyes
I can spot the lies
Inside your insecure
And you're not very sure
But take it someplace
Where I can't see your face
Because you'll only kill
To satisfy your will
And I'll be glad
When I've finally had
A look at you
The real you.

Flip; Flippy; Flippant

Flip, flippy, flippant
Sort of comes off kind of hippant.
Flip: a trick in the air,
Subtlety, mixed with a touch of flair.
Flippy: performed on the ground;
Action carried out, gets all around.
Flippant; sort of high class term,
All of the above, but add a little squirm.
Give a wiggle, give a jiggle, an up and down shake
Look it's blondie! And you thought it was a quake.
It's flip, flippy, flippant,
And she's coming this way
With a smile and that giggle
To make your day.

He Was Never Really Here

He's gone
But he was never really here
And he kind of still is

He's in my heart
But he should have been gone
I don't want him here anymore

But I can't give him up
So I'll keep him here
Even though he's gone

It was too good to be true
I never got him
But I'll keep him

Now he's gone
But he was never really here
And he kind of still is.

The Stray Cats

The cats go stray
And Slim is Jim
There's a song of love
To satisfy my whim

My blood moves even faster
To that rockabilly sound
The ambitious tunes
That only this group has found

The baby sweetness of Brian
Makes it worth cryin'
The mystique of Lee Rocker
Provokes a pleasant shocker

Together they capture
A sound of the past
And they'll keep it going
To make it last.

For The Last Time

Your head's so high
Your mind is a trick
Your scheme has worn
And it leaves you sick

We'll see for the last time
How well you climb
We'll see at the last brawl
How well you crawl

And don't let me raise
My blood pressure any higher
Just one minute more, babe
You'll be running from fire

You've torn and scratched
But you won't get away
Oh yes, you'll be included
On that very special day.

Rays

Run to the rays of the sun
Absorb the kindness it gives
Stand in the light of the rays
Embrace the warmth that lives

Run to the rays of the sun
Enlighten the heart that slows
Reach for a piece of life
That's not too hot, but glows.

A Picnic For Two

A picnic for two
With roses and wine
Just me and you
Covered by sunshine

All day long
Gazing at the sky
A world where we belong
Never wondering why

Strawberry cheesecake
As bright as our love
Fresh baked bread
With crumbs to feed a dove

A perfect picture
A picnic for two
Wouldn't be as wonderful
Unless I was with you.

Let's Talk Brother

We can all survive
We can all come alive
We can all help each other
Let's talk, Brother

We can all open our ears
And listen to each other's fears
We can all fight for each other
So let's talk, Brother

We can all move closer
If we don't understand
We can all link together
Every single hand by hand

And we'll all make it
Being helped by each other
Won't have to fake it,
We got you, Brother.

Candlelight

A tall slender candle
Keeps on burning
My heart in its sleep
Keeps on turning

For a moment, the light
Can be blown out
For a second, the beat
Can be drowned out

Give it some air
To burn out alone
Give me some space
For the heart to be known.

Color Me Red

Color me red
And watch me turn green
Give me a syllable
And watch what I mean

Color me red
It glows in my head
Step over that crack
You'll be heading back
Show me a finger
And run through the ringer
Jump to a scene
Hey, you're turning green!

Color me red
Don't forget to think twice
Give me a syllable
And watch me fix the price

Now look at my eyes
Scanning for lies
What a color -- is red;
Did you hear what I said?

Calm

Calm as the cricket on the porch
That scrambles when you call;
A flicker, in your eyes like a torch
Burning down the trees that were so tall

Calm as the heart of a rat
That beats for survival in the night
Always scrambling for a piece of calm
Deciding between the many sides of right

For only a moment, all is calm
Search the world, sail the sea;
Put a quarter in an old man's palm
Find a place and rest -- for me.

Icecream

As I sit alone
In the summer heat
Drained from emotion
Sharp pains in my feet

Something would be nice
To sweeten a lost dream
Nothing cools me better
Than sweet-lovin' icecream

The icecream that you gave me
Melted away so fast
I knew that something so tender
Could never really last

Now I'll settle for some hard candy
Although that's not my dream
I just can't seem to get a hold
Of that sweet-lovin' icecream.

One

We can be one
If we listen and touch
We can understand
Without saying much

We can be partners
If we walk the same line
We can share each other
Mine is yours; yours mine

We can be one
Tie together our ends
We can be one
More than just friends.

One Light

One light in the dark
May strike a subtle spark
To glow throughout the hallway
And bring sunshine on a rainy day

One light not as strong
Shadowing all that's wrong
All so that we may see
The light of a world so free

One light that shines alone
Just enough to get us home
Where day is warm and sincere
And love is always very near.

Reality

Reality is anything
The state of mind acknowledges
Anything we feel
Can be real
Our eyes have feeling
As well as our hearts
And we know it's real
Because emotion starts
Life is not an illusion
We live it
We give it
Go ahead and touch life
It's all very real
It produces and resembles
Everything we feel.

Wrinkles

The ink in my pen
Remembers when
Paper was smooth.

Help

To understand
Is to fall off the mountain with me
To help
Is to land before I do and catch me.

We are

We are
The Team
To Dream
For

No Trace

There's no trace
Of white lace
On black curtains.

Warm

Warm places
And warm faces
Keep me cool.

Thinking About You

Standing on the tower above
Thinking about love
Thinking about you

Sitting at the top of the highest tree
Thinking about being free
Thinking about you

Bathing in a cool mountain river
Thinking, while I shiver
Thinking about you

A million years in hours
And still holding on to the powers
Of being with you.

The Tree

This is the tree
That stands for me
Because when I'm weak
It stays tall and sleek
It's there for me to lean on
And rest my soul upon
It offers me hope
When my heart can't seem to cope

This is the tree
That was planted for me
And was used by someone yesterday
Who feels a lot better today.

That Piercing Sound of Anger

That piercing sound of anger
That could only be so quiet
Exerts a form of tranquility
And starts a silent riot

I'll hear it for a moment
Then cotton can put it asleep
That piercing sound of anger
That cuts me and makes me weep

I try to soothe the vibration
But it gets louder as you scheme
That piercing sound of anger
Could shatter a glass-made dream

Such walls will never shield me
From the hysteria all around
But what would I learn from any of it
If anger had not a sound.

Sensations

You gave me sensations
That have already passed
Through millions of generations

When I received them
They felt good as new
Because they came from you.

The Small Part

There's a small part left
Of my heart to give away
I'm saving it for someone special
That smiles for me today

It's a very sacred part
That I've kept hidden for so long
It's my only piece of heart
That no one has done wrong

The rest is withered and gray
That minds have exhausted in a year
But I hope it comes alive today
When I find the smile so sincere

There's a small part left
Of my heart to give away
A part I've held forever
Until I found you today

In your hands, you hold the breath
From that small part of my destination
And if one finger slips loose
I'll have only anticipation.

In My Sleep

And in my sleep
I've only a dream to keep
Of the vision you portray
Moving farther and farther away

My reach is extended
To the farthest point possible
But the misty illusion disappears
Out of sight 'til it's only a blur
Leaving me with all the fears

Of sleeping in darkness
With an edge on each side
Bearing surprises for me to uncover
And foolishly squawking at my ignorance
Of the unknown in his soul
That puts on a fake performance

And in my sleep
There'll be treasures I'll keep
To hide in the part of my heart
That's still a sacred, worthy part

But I'll remember when I wake
The threads of my life you had to take
Realizing when I weep
That I was not at all asleep.

Pink

The pink of it all
Is that it's funny
How kisses are worthy
Of so much money

If you believe they are
They'll be harder to give
If you believe they're gifts
Then give them and live.

Ice

My hands feel like ice
Cold
From the hold
That's not present

My heart feels like ice
Pale
From the jail
I've been locked up in

Melting
Slowly
With time
But still cold
From the hold.

Ideas

There's nothing more to say
It's all been said
There's a lot more to do
Than keep ideas in my head.

Heaters

If only my hands were heaters
We'd all be warmed
By a friendly touch

My hands are always cold
But everyone I touch
Everyone I smile at
Receives a little warmth
A warmth that comes
From the heart
The heater in my heart
That is much warmer
Than the heater in people's hands;
Mine even works in summer.

Wave Goodbye

I don't want to watch this
I don't want to sit here
I want to go to a place
They talk about
In the sky
And wave goodbye
To the place existing
Which is no place at all
But only exists
As a foundation for the place
They talk about
In the sky
And wave goodbye
To the friends I had
Which are no friends at all
But only exist
As supporters for the place
They talk about
In the sky
And I'll wave goodbye
To everything.

A Stab

Are you gonna take that back?
What you put in my back
And then you ran from the sight of blood
Because you couldn't handle it
But you came back
To push it in even farther.

The Subtle Dance

The subtle dance
Puts me in a trance
Then I can't see
Anything around me
Lovers look like they're in a trance
But they don't dance
They just don't appreciate
How lucky they are.

Prison

They say that
Prisoners have it easy
Food, bed, clothes
Not having to worry about money
It's the damn walls
And the freak calls
That make 'em go crazy.

A Shake

A shake
It must have happened at night
Everything was quiet
But something wandered
Wandered out the door
And never existed anymore
That's why I'm happy.

Life Rope

Okay, so I saw this rope
I grabbed it and started climbing
To see where it would go
So then I started sweatin'
And was almost at the end
When somebody cut it
I know 'cause they threw
A big pair of scissors on my head.

Never

Never will I
dream of you
Never
because there wouldn't
be a clear picture
Never will I
talk to you
Never, ever
There wouldn't be
anything to say
Never will I
look or listen
Never, ever
because it just
makes me cry
after I talk to you
and you never
ever
talk to me
first.

Wrapped Around a White Silk Sheet

Wrapped around
A white silk sheet
Like a cocoon
We discover each other
Under the moon

The ground is cold
But we keep warm
In each other's hold

This is love
That cannot be undone
Because under the silk sheet
We are one

One, because of our devotion
And not merely delight
Our whole-hearted emotion
Keeps our love right

Wrapped around
A white silk sheet
Not an inch between us
Our hearts sincerely meet

The ground is cold
But we keep warm
In each other's hold.

The Sun

As I sit here, staring out the window
I wonder about the sun
The sun that knows no sadness
But portrays the color of smiles
Smiles, that cover up madness

I sit here yearning to grab
A piece of the sun
To warm my heart
That's been taken apart

As I sit here
With the warmth on my shoulder
I think about my health
More important than any wealth
And I smile

I smile knowing that my heart
Will recover very soon
Then I will glow just like the sun
And be thankful for what it's done.

Fire

Sparks dash
In a flash
Through the air
Against any dare

The burning flame
Will play the game
Of a peaceful dance
That places a trance

Water burns
When the fire turns
Like a laser beam
Captivating a dream

Fire is the heart
It is the center spirit
And when I dance
You'll be able to hear it.

Interest

Interest is only what it means
You pay for what you borrow
And all that's left is sorrow

Interest is a nudge on your hip
A warm touch on the arm
A twinkling eye for charm

Interest is only what it means
It may go left, it may go right
Interest is only what it means;
Borrowed for the night.

Another Way

If you have found
Another way
Draw me a map
And start to pray
If I get there tomorrow
Wait on the track
If I find it next week
Show me how to get back.

Get To You

I see you
And you see me
But I'll get to you
Before you leave

I read your eyes
And what they need
Is a new surprise
For your soul to be freed

I'll get to you somehow
In more ways than you know
I'll get to you
Then you won't want to go.

The Maiden

Every time the doorbell rings
There is no one at the door
Every time the maiden sings
I clap and ask for more
Every time a bird is born
It does not want to fly
Every time I fall on a thorn
The maiden lets me cry
When all the geese fly south
They remember their natural home
When the maiden quietly enters
She writes me a powerful poem
Every time the doorbell rings
The mailman will have gone by
But every time the maiden sings
She leaves me with a sigh
And when she leaves
She cannot be heard
But as her gift to me
Is this page of words.

Wrinkles (2)

Yes, there were wrinkles
But the paper's stretched tight
It's still not perfect
But it's much easier to write.

A Rose Knows

A rose knows
Where it gets its red
But can the heart interpret
What the red has said?

The red from love
Is love from above
Can a heart be red
From mere words you have said?

Give me a rose
Still planted in the ground
Then I will know
If real red can be found.

Along the Blazing Trail

Along the blazing trail
Even love will prevail
Because what is already hot
Will never burn 'til it's not

Plastic will melt and wood will char
Gold will run like bubbling tar
Leaves will drip and fabric will dry
But does not the smoke drift up to the sky?

To the sky where it lives
And with the cool air it gives
Because what is already hot
Will never burn 'til it's not.

Let's Thank God

Let's thank God
For the laughter he brings
For the sensitivity and humor
That makes up life's strings

Let us not forget
Our place is to share
The joys and pains
With others everywhere

We are not for ourselves
But for others to trust
Let's thank God
If we believe, we must

If we believe in the good
We must spread it with pride
Because it will come back to us
So that everyone may confide

Let's thank each other
And learn to love and give
We are here to learn together
And together we must live.

The Maple Tree

Lime, auburn, and yellow
Dripping on the stubby fellow
Who's sleeping with his magazine
Under the old maple tree

One lime leaf falls, slap!
Right on the fellow's lap
Who's sleeping with his magazine
Under the old maple tree

One auburn leaf floats, weeee!
Right on the old man's knee
Who's sleeping with his magazine
Under the old maple tree

One leaf that's a happy yellow
Lands right on the nose of the fellow
Who then walks over with his magazine
Under another maple tree.

The Cold

The cold
Is coming
The bitter cold
With snow and ice
And a temperature that's bold
The cold, the cold
That puts us all indoors
The bitter cold
That freezes our floors
And cools our beds
And reddens our noses
The bitter cold
That kills the pretty roses
The cold, the cold
Is coming.

That Picture

Why do we have that picture up there?
All he does is sulk and stare
Where's the truth?
Where's the proof?
Why do we have it hanging up there?
Can't it be stored in a box somewhere?
I don't understand
What's been painted by hand
Where's the truth?
And where's the proof?

Two Feet Away

Two feet away
But farthest from my mind
Just stay two feet away
And I'll be rid of your kind

Not an inch will make a difference
Not a step will make me give in
The more you try to come closer
The farther I will keep runnin'

Stand there in the dark
Just two feet away
Because for my dear life
To God, I will pray.

The Brightest Star

When the brightest star in the sky
Shines so bright it makes me cry
And when the leaves of Fall drift down
So gracefully they erase my frown
You will know that I am alive
And not just living.

Mira's Play

Mira, in the garden of Eden
Runs from an apparition
She falls over a partition
And discovers the other side
Mira, who's never been elsewhere
Starts to face the illusion
And comes up with a conclusion
That this is where lovers hide
She picks every flower in sight
And notices a strange, skinny pose
Not knowing she has picked a rose
That a man gives to his bride
So Mira pretends to be Juliet
Unties her hair and reveals her grace
Leaving only the blankets of mother's lace
That she keeps for sake of pride
Out of the shadows comes Romeo
What a figure, what an arm, no simplicity
They touch and form sparks of electricity
A sure song of hearts being tied
Then Juliet trips, oh terribly too!
She drops the rose in a puddle that's blue
After retrieving it, she turns to Romeo
But he has disappeared is all she seems to know
She looks at the rose which is red no more
A dizziness overcomes her and she drops to the floor
Mira throws the rose away
And walks out of her play
Deciding that it is finer
To stay in her life as a minor.

Laughing Up the Stairs

Someone's knocking
The house is rocking
My sisters are mocking
And I'm laughing down the stairs

The door is opening
Someone is offering
My sisters are loitering
And I'm laughing down the stairs

In he is walking
Someone is squawking
My sisters are talking
And I'm laughing down the stairs

Ha-ha-ha
It's a riot
He looks at me
My sisters are quiet

Ha-ha-ha
He's taken me with him
My sisters are grinnin'
And I'm still laughin'
All the way up the stairs.

Winning

I'm glad I don't hear you anymore
I'm glad you're hiding underneath my floor
There won't be all those faces
Of you disguised in so many places
Everyone's uncovered your deadly truth
Well - when you left behind all the proof!
I'm glad you live behind those curtains
They are as black as your soul
I'm glad you talk to yourself now
There's no one else there in your hole

I guess I've waited for it to come to this
You were afraid to admit it all along
Can't you just shoot yourself dead
Knowing, now, that you were wrong?
Oh, you know I won't help you now
Should have thought of that in the beginning
I remember distinctly how you felt
And you kept telling me you were winning.

A Garden Full of Roses

Let me guide you through
That garden full of roses
I know the way through
I know all that it proposes

Let me take you by hand
So that you'll feel at ease
I know all that it possesses
And how it wishes to please

It's just a garden of roses
Planted only for what is true
And by looking at us together
It has to be for me and you

I water it every morning
So they never will go dry
Each and every rose
Has a heart that will never die

Let me show you the way
To that very last rose
I know the way through
I know what it will propose.

Rain

And with the snow
Comes rain, rain
Rain that falls like pain

And when the sun burns
The rain will cool like rain
Rain that falls like pain

And when the sun and cold win
I'll get up on the highest pole
And wait for the rain, rain
With my knife I'll kill the pain
Pain that hits like rain.

To The Brightest Eyes

To the brightest eyes I've ever seen
I give my smile and all that it will mean
The smile to make them even brighter
And to look upon things even lighter
To the brightest eyes that have looked at me
And made me wonder what they see
To eyes that only speak with grace
And move me with the shine on his face
To the brightest eyes that speak so fine
I give my smile and all that's seen in mine.

Little Black Slippers

I will pull on
My little black slippers
And conquer the world.

For Me

This one is for you
All that you do
This tear is for you
All you've been through

This is for your smile
That they have ripped
This is for the beat
That your heart has skipped

This is for your voice
Hoarse and dry
This gives you a choice
No other than to cry.

Let Myself Sing

I'll let myself sing
Sing to dying people
I'll let myself sing
Sing to the sky above

And all of life will know
That all it takes to grow
Is a hand and a smile
Just be back in a while
To hear me sing

I'll sing for the people
Sing for your friends
Sing for the stars above
And I'll sing 'til it ends

How can I sing from these tears?
Tears that shout from anger
How must I sing from these tears?
Tears that flow for you

Why does it rain on my house?
Why don't the birds sing with me?
I'll let myself hear them
I'll let myself be them
But I'll let myself sing
Sing to me.

Fear

Now I'll show my fear
When all that's right is near
I'll let myself sing
I'll show this feeling
Because I know
I know what it is to try
Try so hard, sweat and cry
I know what it is to hold
To hold onto a pulse and be bold
And I know what it is to feel
Feel something fake and believe it's real
But I've learned
I've learned that the voice is to yell
And my eyes are to water and watch
My hands are to pound in a cell
And my heart is to serve as a blotch
A big red blotch
That seems to have no place
A big red blotch
That beats without a trace
But they are wrong
All, all, all, all wrong
Just look deeper and you'll see
The fire whistling inside of me
And see that I really know
And see that I've really learned.

Run Again

No problem -
I'll just have to get back up again,
Straighten out my legs and then,
Run like I always did.

For You, Grandma

This I will dedicate
To the one I love
This is for the person
Who gives me all her love

She may be old
But she tells me no lies
And nothing warms me better
Than that look in her eyes

She holds me very tight
And I know by her touch
That every little feeling
Means she loves me very much

No one is like my grandmother
Who has seen and has taught me
I love her more than anything
And I will, eternally

For all she's done and helped me through
I owe my life and all I know
And this poem is only a small token
Of the love for her I wish to show.

Mimi

She is a doll
Skinny and sweet
Wearing knitted skirts
And socks rolled neat

Bobby brown hair
Hanging up to her chin
Sparkling little eyes
That I see myself in

Nothing could be nicer
Than this doll of mine
Mimi always makes me smile
And keeps me feeling fine.

Mr. Right

Excuse me,
I'm looking for Mr. Right
Have you seen him yet?
He said he'd be here tonight

He's wearing nice clothes
And that cologne I simply adore
Have you seen him yet?
Is he on the dance floor?

Oh, he's a pretty good height
Of course he has dark hair
Have you seen him yet?
I've been looking everywhere

Yeah, he smiles a lot
And is surely real polite
Are you sure you didn't see him
Walking through that door tonight?

Of course I'm sure he's Mr. Right
My feelings never lie
The only proof I really have
Is my dazed and amazed sigh

Oh, there he is, excuse me
This one I'm gonna keep
He's fine, he's mine, it's like a dream
But this time I'm not asleep.

If I Write

If I write
I'll sleep easier tonight
If I write sorrow
I'll be over it tomorrow.

Something, Anything

Think of something,
Anything
To fill up pages in a book

Think of anything,
Something
To disturb that half-dazed look

Think of something
That scratches and calls
While the wind is blowing
Against those walls

Think of anything
That makes you blush
While walking through
The morning rush

Think of something
Don't you know?
Does it come to your mind
What I'm trying to show?

Think of anything
I'll wait here all day
Does it come to your mind
What I'm trying to say?

I Haven't Even Begun

I've sat in the middle
For quite a while
I've sat there and waited
Trying to force a smile

But I haven't even begun
So why do I complain
I haven't even felt it
So why do I blame

I'm only in the middle
At the age of seventeen
I haven't even begun
To understand what it means

And here I am, whining
About something I do not know
I haven't even begun
Yet I want my doubts to show

I haven't even begun
To be fooled or betrayed
Yet I sit here and bleed
From an invisible blade

Truly, truly mistaken
At the age of sixteen and one
I haven't even felt it
I haven't even begun.

The Happening

The happening,
It is a glistening
In the eyes

The happening,
It is an enlightening
In the heart

The happening,
It is a welcoming
In the arms

The happening,
It is an accomplishment
By the accomplisher.

One Man

One man who I wish to be dead
Because of all he puts in my head
One man who makes me choke when near
Because he always insists that I hear
One man who makes me mentally ill
Because my ideas he wishes to kill
One man who I will never remember
And will always regret on the 28th of September.

Our Barn

I wish I could live in our barn
It is behind our house
It is very quiet and dusty.

Ears

My ears do throb
My mind does pound
I'll never rest soundly
'Til I'm buried in the ground.

Ruby-Red Nails

Claw-like
And ruby-red
Filed round
Blunt instead

But claw-like
To pick details
Filed round
Ruby-red nails.

On A Hill

On a hill of sunny dandelions
Looking up at the sky
No one would ever see me
If I were to die

If I sat there 'til tomorrow
If I sat there 'til midnight
No one would ever see me
If I supposedly were to die

On a hill of sunny dandelions
Writing verses for the sun
No one would ever read me
No one would know I was done

So I won't sit 'til tomorrow
And I will leave before midnight
Because there's nobody on that hill
To stand and watch me die.

When It Rains

The sky is green
The trees are blue
And when it rains
I think of you

I think of what we say when we meet
And how you look down at your feet
You always do when I come by
You always do when I say "hi"

I think of all we care to say
It keeps repeating in my head all day
I'll never hear it once more, but then
I look forward until we meet again.

From The Moment

From the moment that I started
All my senses had departed
And the only thing for me now
Is to break that splintering vow

From the day my eyes awakened
I felt I had been mistaken
And I can throw what I used to keep
Hidden inside me, oh, so deep

From the moment that I started
I knew I'd end up broken-hearted
And the only thing for me to do now
Is to live by an honest vow.

In Place of Face

To send a card
In place of face
Makes it hard
To see the real response

To mail a letter
In place of face
Couldn't be better
Than the honest response

To ring a word
In place of face
Will not be heard
As a true response

To knock at the door
And see face to face
The best real response
Is a friend's embrace.

Love, So Free

To the soul that brings about a tear
And leaves for me the world to fear
To love, mistakenly displayed with grace
Which causes the tear that flows down my face

May all the world see I am blind
Because I stand to speak and remind
Of all the grief that love can carry
And drop at once in the ground to bury

To all it has been, but a lovely mess
And prove upon me foolish distress
Because it never leaves nor lets me be
That soul that promised love so free

Eating away at my heart so red
And leaving the breathing piece instead
Why didn't it take that too
But only left me here with you

And I can only watch faithfully
At what should have happened to love so free
Making me wonder about my state
Leading me to figure out my fate

To air and ground and all I see
Why are they real, but not love so free?
Shall I wait before midnight and hold my breath?
Sooner or later I will feel, yet before my death

Of all the great poets, not one I know
Will tell me why this pain will not go
And I just wonder in agony
What has become of a love so free.

Always and Always

And I will always;
Because of what I knew of you
And because of what I admire
There will always be a tender spark
And always a burning fire

And I will always;
Because of how you played to me
And stayed with me a while
There will always be a charming glow
And always a friendly smile

And I will always;
Always and always;
Don't ask me why.

The Light of Day

By the light of day
Should I go astray
Light a candle
And leave before it burns out

By the fall of night
Should I lose my sight
Light a candle
And leave before it burns out

You always run
After you light it
I wish you'd stay
And help me fight it

I guess you do
Because there's no time to cry
It's only that I wish
You'd stop and say goodbye

If at any day
You should walk my way
And not care to say a word

Keep walking without a sound
And hurt will not be found
If your presence cannot be heard.

My Room

My room is dim
My walls are gray
My face is white
Because the sun is far away

It shines far from my window
And leaves my room dim
It doesn't give me happiness
But leaves my life grim

What would happen
If it shone on my walls?
Would it brighten my room
Or just darken my halls?

What would happen
If I opened the curtain?
Would it make me smile
Would it stop my hurting?

My room just keeps dim
My walls are ever-gray
And I keep hoping
The sun will enter one day.

Change

Change from one to another
Change from father to mother
Change from goat to dog
Change from smoke to fog
Change from coat to hat
Change from mouse to rat
Change from cover to sheet
Change from wind to heat
Change from smile to stare
Change from common to rare
Change from crow to dove
Change from hate to love.

Still I Wonder

And still I wonder
About God's thunder
And about the worthless
How it acts so painless

Still I wonder
And wonder, and wonder
About a friendly kiss
About people I miss
About a walk in the rain
About the crying from pain

Oh, it makes me wonder
And wonder and wonder
How an old man stands
How lovers hold hands
How a walk in the rain
Makes me forget about pain

But I'll always wonder
And wonder and wonder
How after you read this
You'll pretend never to miss
The sharing of a friendly kiss
And how you'll walk in the rain
Never crying out in pain. . .
   from wonder

Do you ever wonder
About God's thunder?
Is it a message he gives
For people like you and me?

How The Kitchen Rug Lays

What does it matter
How the kitchen rug lays
It is not its position
That in the future pays

What does it matter
When I walk down the aisle
Will you bring it in
For a laugh or a smile?

What the hell will it matter
After I'm living on my own
Making the best of my life
And being independent from home

Is it a test if you love me
To see that I lay it straight
It won't matter after you've pushed me
Out the door, and it's too late.

Once

There was once a silent night
When the stars shone very bright
There was not a finer moon ever
And it seemed like it would shine forever.

A Gift of Gold

Here's a gift of gold
Which you would rather hold
Next to your heart

Here's a gift of lace
Which you would rather place
Next to your heart

But I ask you sincerely
And please answer dearly
Does the gold give you warmth?
Does the lace give you comfort?

Here's a gift of telecommunication
Which you may use to notify me
When the gold starts to warm you
And when the lace starts to comfort you

Until then, live your life sincerely
And think of me dearly.

On Pink Paper

On pink paper
I live my life
On pastel sheets
I write my soul

On pretty leaflets
I spell my dreams
On light colored prints
I work on my goal

On pink paper
I imagine all
On pastel sheets
No idea is quite small

On a line of gray
I act out a play
I write all the words
That I'm afraid to say.

A Moment

T'was a moment which exerted
A force that was much blurted
But escaped before I was able
To cut off a circuit in the main cable

T'was a moment that must be forgotten
Since it came out so undeserving
Believe not a word what you read before
But keep enjoying the thoughts I'm reserving.

From a Picture

From a picture I cried
It touched me at the center
From a feeling from the picture
All my thoughts I denied

I held it oh so long
And felt everything I could
I held it oh so tightly
And knew it was all wrong

From a picture I cried
And said I'd never look twice
From the feeling from the picture
The thoughts sure were nice.

If Someone Would Sing

How I wish someone would sing a song
  Of the verses I write so strong
What music that would be
  And I would enjoy it immensely

How I wish I had a piano to play
  The music I write on paper every day
What music that would be
  Something from inside of me

How I wish someone would dance
  To the lyrics I've written by chance
What a step that would be
  For all other dancers to see

How I wish a song could be sung
  From the words of a fool
What music that would be
  And what would that tell you?

Expressions

If at all you try to read me
Then I'd be afraid you wouldn't need me
If my expressions are a blur
It's only to protect me by being obscure

If at all you try to read me
Try to understand where I'm from
And if you decide that you still need me
Wait at my front door and I'll come.

So Soon

So soon you go away
Not even one more day

So soon the laughter ends
Since we've become such good friends

So soon you go away
It's because of me you won't stay

So soon the laughter ends
But we'll always be good friends

I'd rather swing with you watching
Instead of pushing
And we'd stay friends longer if
So soon you'd go away.

Foolish Distress

My ink is full of foolishness
'Cuz all it writes is foolish distress
Maybe it's time I got a new pen
Maybe it will all change, but when?

From where does such misery flow
To spot on my paper and show?
Maybe it's time to type in ink
Maybe it's time to change, I think

Is it the way I hold my tool
That, on paper, makes me seem a fool?
Is it the ink, so black and shiny
That uncovers all defects, even so tiny?

Maybe I will get a new pen
Maybe it'll all change by then
But where will I put my foolishness?
Where will I hide my foolish distress?

A Silent Song

What mood does winter bring?
A silent song that all birds sing
What mood does chill the air outside?
Where in the snow do the warm spots hide?

Hidden deep below the icy layer
My thoughts awaken with a prayer
And only God can hear me now
Only God can hear me now.

The Stage

What's happening to the stage?
Is the structure falling apart?
It's not that sturdy old stage
On which actors acted from the heart

What's happening to its wood?
All splintered, peeled and gray
It's not that shiny, smooth wood
That from the heart the actors did play

What's happening?
What's happening?
Why don't you humor me anymore?
Like your smile did before
Why don't you talk to me that way?
'So fine is life', you used to say

But what's happening now?
To the stage we used to live on
The stage we used to love on

Now I'm sitting in the audience
Watching with true-blood confidence
How good an actor you are.

Ask

You always have to ask
To be sure
You always have to remind
To feel secure.

Born

Just like when you first wake up
You feel like you were just born...
slow, raw, dumb

And even if you feel that way at other times
You can be sure to start it over
And try it differently.

(untitled)

For all it seems to be
He may turn to your sister
For all you've dreamt to see
You'll know he hasn't missed her

If it seems out of mind
That he should be with you
Then your sister is so lucky
To have him, too

What a ludicrous thought
But isn't everything the same?
Just when you had him marked
He calls you your sister's name

It only explains the truth
In false feelings being mixed
And if you wait, you will know
The right one with whom you'll be fixed.

Drama

Like silence will speak
Like the strong become weak
Like people can play
And be fools for a day
The drama prevails in all
It makes us human
It changes our fate
And even for some, can bring death
The drama colors clowns
It decides the happy endings
It translates our words
And even for some, can bring truth
The drama is in the houses
Between fathers and daughters
Daughters - they wish were sons
The drama is in the schools
Between teachers and students
Students - they wish were scholars
The drama is in the churches
Between relatives and friends
Friends - they wish were far away
But silence is so loud when it isn't heard
And even the words unspoken can hurt
Especially if those words are from actors we call friends
Especially if those words lack feeling
Only a good actor can live the drama
Until he cannot control the silence
Then, even he, will become weak
With drama, his age will wither
And his tongue will become limp
But, oh, the drama in everyday people
They think they fool us
And if we turn away, they frown
Because we supposedly offend them
Ha! Such good actors should take criticism!
Then they may improve on their smiles
Their careers need training to be foolproof
Then the drama won't easily fade away

It is the life, love, and spirit that will
But drama brings them wealth and prosperity
It gives them security and warmth
It gives them hope for tomorrow
Drama keeps them in relation with us
Drama puts them high on a pedestal
For all to see, admire, and honor
Drama gets them prestige and popularity
If they are ever to succeed, they must act
And to act, they must imply, restate and disillude
For if we knew who they really were
They would hide; maybe refuse to speak
They'll grow tired of smiling and pretending
Their drama will fade away
Along with their spirit
And clowns will grow pale

Like silence will become deafening
Like the weak will become strong
The people will be afraid to play
And fools will be fools
Like we already are
All of us.

Paradise

So far by the edge of hope
And not sure how much longer to cope
It flew from the sky
Swept me up, oh so high
And left me in true, blue paradise

I guess it was scary at first
But after I had quenched my thirst
I felt refreshed
Knew I'd been blessed
And discovered how lovely is paradise.

In the Company of a Bore

At last our eyes had wonderingly met
At last our smiles exchanged hearts
We found ourselves only inches apart, yet
Words would barely start

I had the greeting memorized and he did, too
But we waited for something else to come
Small comments, he had said a few
That I had never felt so dumb

The floor was an interesting concept
The ceiling was also attractive
But the two of us had nothing to say
And when I did, he was non-reactive

I found myself in the company of a bore
And fiddled, smiled and swayed
I realized I could not take it anymore
But to leave, I was afraid

Afraid, to leave him alone in his boredom
When I could share myself with him
Pausing between things to say
Just to keep the topic fresh
Even though he responded coldly
To every word I said
I knew one thing for sure
I left him thinking.

When She Yells

It's so hard on my mind
When my mother yells
It's so hard to be kind
When she yells, yells, yells

If she'd only think for a moment
Before breaking up in terror
If she'd only know how prevalent
Is her common parental error

If she'd only hear me out
And stop growling like a wolf
I'd make it all seem simpler
And she need not blow the roof

If I should ever meet a witch
Would I be able to relate
Would I think of my mother
And what images would I create

It's terribly hard on my mind
When my mother yells
It's so hard to be kind
When she yells, yells, yells!

Now What?

Just when it all seems fair
And when it's finally time to smile
The bad comes back from nowhere
To haunt me for the while

Who wants to get me now?
As if I'm rid of all my hate
Who wants to kill me now?
That has carried it out so late
It might as well be finished
Since no one can see through
My excitement's been diminished
And now my strategies are few

Everyone's complaining about what's right
But I'm stuck with all that's wrong
And they can't appreciate their happiness
When I've been waiting for it so long

Just when it all seems so fair
It's down to a thousand against one
And if I don't hold on through it
It'll keep killing 'til I'm done.

By the Way

By the way
I just came to say
How much I love you

I know it's been a while
But I haven't forgotten the smile
That we shared alone

You've probably changed
But I haven't re-arranged
The love I have for you

I just happened to look out today
And I knew I had to say
How much I love you

I just wanted you to know
That my love for you still grows
Because it's one good thing I share
With you; a friend so very rare

And I wouldn't let this go by
Without even saying "hi"
I wouldn't have passed right through
Without saying "I love you!"

Spring is Me

Spring is me
So fresh and young
Waiting to be uncovered
Waiting to absorb sunshine

Spring is me
So cool and sweet
Full of newborn color
Full of beauty so innocent

Spring is me
So quiet yet expressive
Blooming with smiling flowers
Blooming with vivid joy

Spring is all in me
And I am all in Spring
The simplicity of senses
The glory of reactions

The beauty in the forgotten ones
Comes alive at Spring time
There's a freshness from within
That lets the beauty of youth begin.

Being Young

Maybe I should have waited
For the sun to rise
For the glow in your eyes
For the tale of the wise

It would have been much easier
To know the place
To recognize the face
To finish the race

Maybe I should have waited
'Til I grew up
'Til I was free
'Til I could speak

Then I would know what I was speaking about.

Mr. B

Mr. B was here
And he said I looked so fine
Mr. B had fooled me
Because he would not be mine

He flirted with a fancy
He touched and made me "ill"
I asked him if he'd like me
But he never said "I will"

Mr. B went his way
And I alone went mine
But Mr. B, remember me
Even if you can't be mine.

The Borderline

Lurking alongside the borderline
Is a monster called Fate
He waits for the moments so fine
And his rewards never come late

Hanging on the edge of the borderline
Is an old chap called Trust
He expects only deeds so fine
And he rewards all that he must

Clinging to the side of the borderline
Is a brother we all know as love
He expects nothing but a smile so fine
And his rewards all come from above.

God Forbids Me

God forbids me to write
Silliness
God forbids me to write

He only allows truthfulness
He only allows hopefulness

And I can try as hard as hell
For my grief and misery to spell
But God forbids my persistence
He won't let me destroy my own confidence.

(untitled)

What a fine time
For Spring to come
When I've lifted my spirits
And lightened the burden
And I know the air is new
Because I can stand straight
My lungs expand easier
My eyes shine brighter
And all because Spring
Has brought new feeling into me
To be able to tell you
How I feel
Without making you wonder
And since I have explained
It doesn't bother me anymore
It doesn't haunt me inside
It won't ever live off my heart
All because I've told you
Everything I've ever wanted to tell you
And I can sleep soundly at night
I can smile sincerely by day
I can talk about love
I can laugh with those in line
Because it doesn't bother me
Anymore
And quite frankly
Makes me feel more certain
About the people we are
And the people we can be
We can be anything
And after I talked with you
I'm sure that we can be
Friends.

Maturity

How do people know
When you've grown
And when you've stopped
How do they see
When you have risen
To your highest point
And when you've dropped
How do people realize
When you start loving them
And when you cherish them
How do they honestly know
When your heart beats for them
And you tremble at their touch
And you glow when they're around
How do they know
That your dreams are all in color
That your words are all whispers
That your thoughts are a rainbow
And how do they proceed to know
That you're not just dreaming
That your words are poetic verses
That your thoughts can turn to actions
How do you show
When you've grown up
And when you have risen
How do people honestly know
And how will I ever honestly know
When they never tell me.

My Hand

Even though sometimes my hand
May be so cold and dry
I still want you to take it
I still want you to hold it

And if it starts to get warmer
You can smile for what you've done
It will be warm for always
It will always be warm for you

Even if I hold on tightly
You can push a harder grip
Because I still want you near me
I still want you to hold me

The bravest and the biggest
Have all walked on by
But you have stopped before me
To wipe all my tears dry

If I should ever look upon you
And not see that lucky grin
I shall take your hand in mine
And hold it tightly within.

Out of One

Out of one
And into another
It's good to be
On the other side
Even though sometimes
It's not so perfect
It was never expected to be
But I'm over the line
And still haven't looked back
Because I don't even want to try
All that's important
Is that it's over
I'm out of one
And into another
Even as I wonder
Looking out at the new grass
My heart pulls me forward
And keeps me that way.

(untitled)

I know we've only met
And there's much about me you don't know
But there's time for us to talk
And you should listen before you go

I don't look for much
In a lover or a friend
But I do believe in trying
'Til it takes me to the end

Yes, at first I had watched you
And have been intrigued all along
In your eyes I found no wonder
Whether together we could be strong

I knew I had not been mistaken
When we touched and our hearts met
You brought the smile out from under me
And a feeling I'll never regret

As it all moved along so sincerely
I knew I couldn't be driven away
It felt so good to be by your side
And I hope that together we'll stay.

The Night

But the night
Still brings wonder
And intrigues me by day
The night is always newer
And uncovers strengths
Not found before
Even in day
There's a little night left
That puts me in suspense
About my life
And about others
But the night
Is there for a challenge
And fills me with wonder
To make life interesting
As if it hadn't been.

Who?

Who do you want me to be?
I will ask you
Who is it that you see?
I will ask you
Who is it that you dream of?
I will ask you and ask you again
For never can I be
Who you want me to be
I can only be me

And there is someone
Who wants me as me
He is more welcome by far
Than you and your possessions
He is more favored by far
Than you and your obsessions

And when I would have been
Who you wanted me to be
You ran in circles from confusion
Now I don't see you as anybody
And I'm out of my delusion.

Signals

God hath given me signals
But I ignored them
And now I am hurt
God hath given me whispers
But I refused to acknowledge them
And now I am hurt

God hath offered help
But the help I turned away
And now I beg forgiveness
And 'til I'm forgiven, I will pray

God hath offered strength
But I felt I already was strong
And now I pray for forgiveness
And to never again be wrong

Never again shall I ignore
The signals that could save me
Never again shall I refuse
The whispers that could change me

But now I must suffer the pain
The pain that will bring down tears
Now I will endure the hurt
The hurt that will prove me fierce.

Ode - On a Raindrop that Resembles a Tear

Oh, tiny little raindrop!
Such beauty do you possess
A shiny, silky beauty
That stains a fair-flowered dress

Oh, tiny little body!
Such a heart do you acquire
That beats instead of throbs
For my teardrops to admire

And I hold out my hand
To catch you in the cold
For never will my teardrops
Allow me to behold

So freely do you drop
And then fade away from view
Different from my teardrops
That surround my eyes like dew

Oh, tiny little raindrop!
How I cry to have your soul
For you will always dry up
But my tears continually roll.

Optimism

When there's no sense
In crying
Look up at the sky
And smile about the good things
About little baby chicks
That play around the yard
About how warm the sun shines
On your back while lying in the grass
About the sound of someone's laugh
When you truly make them giggle
About the pictures that were drawn
By your little, little sister

Since there's no sense in crying
Give a lift to your chin
Think about God's wonders
And reward him your grin.

Carry Me Through the Garden

Carry me through the garden
Don't drop me along the way
Just hold me by the hand, my dear
And yours forever I'll stay

Not because you hold me
Not because you're shy
And not because you make me laugh
It's just because you try

So safe and sound I feel with you
You can rest upon my arm
So grand and pretty I feel with you
When you pour me all your charm

Oh! Carry me through the garden
Don't drop me along the way
Just hold me by the hand, my dear
And yours forever I'll stay

You always talk of beautiful roses
And how they bloom full of love
You always share the wonderful dreams
That come to you from above

And when you smile into my eyes
My face becomes all a'glow
There's love! Love! Plenty of love!
And it's love I wish to show

Oh! Carry me through the garden
Don't drop me along the way
Just hold me by the hand, my dear
And yours forever I'll stay.

(untitled)

At such a loss
For words
The page seems plain
The pen seems quiet
For it has always
Written passion or distress
Now the passion's gone
And I'm rid of distress
Thank you, Lord, Almighty
For setting me free.

No Such Word

There's no such word
For all the hurt
All the tears
And all the pain
No such word
Which says it all
Which spells the grief
Which means the same
No such word
Can ever say
The pain that took my heart away
No such word
Can ever show
Why finally now it's time to grow.

Passion

What gave me this passion?
I do not know
But it builds and builds
Until it explodes in flame

What built up this passion
I do not know
But it burns and burns inside me
Until my claws cut into my skin

'Tis not a passion from my gender
Nor a passion of the touch
But an experiment from the devil
That builds it up so much.

A Plea

Why do I cry
And why do I smile
Which comes first and which comes last
I have much to say
But my mother doesn't listen
I have much love
But my mother turns away
Accusations make me laugh
And praise makes me cry
My mother has re-arranged them
And she'll never explain why
I did not grow up in a jungle
I did not just climb off a boat
I am not a computerized robot
And I am not as stiff as a tree
How many times can I listen
And listen, and listen to shrill
How many times can I think of a reason
But find no chance to explain

Dear, dear Mother
I love you with my might
But you've turned away my soul
And now I wish to die.

Inner Confusion

When all around me is fine
And overhead the sky is clear
Explain the inner confusion
Explain why I am here

When roses bloom in Summer
And the rain feels good in Spring
Explain the inner confusion
Explain this cold feeling

Nothing has been solved
But this is the last one for today
I bid regards to all my friends
The friends who have turned me away

These passing little phrases
Of every kind of fear
Make life a great big wonder
And nothing seems so near

With the last bit of hope
That could ever be drained from me
I live in God's own justice
And I live in eternal peace.

Recurring Dream

Why must I dream
To find the room with the gold
What is there left in my room
When there's nothing to hold

Why must I close my eyes
To see visions of joy
My parents even say it
I should have been a boy

Beyond my window
There are fresh green spirits
And I stare out all day
For my heart to hear it

There's a vine of roses
Growing out of my reach
And there's a wild man running
Running, on a moon-lit beach

His heart pounds with his feet
As he runs from the fire
There's a young girl hanging ahead
Loosely, by a wire

The sea moves in on him
And his body becomes the sea
Washing away the shores of the world
I notice, he looks like me

In so long, not a verse would come
For my thoughts had dried of fear
Anxiety builds up quietly
And an explosion seems to be near

But the sea always drowns it
And the fire always burns
There's a dream I keep forever
That inside my room churns

And the door cannot open
Unless touched by human hands
If it should close forever
Watch me swing from heavenly strands.

Many Starry Nights

There isn't a love greater
Than the love I have for you
And my smile gets brighter and brighter
As I think of all you do

Many times I've dreamt
For this day which is finally mine
The wait was quite worth it
Because the feelings sure are fine

And many starry nights went by
As I thought of you through tears
But now the finest night is glowing
The best it's been in years

How such a touch could trigger
Every power to light up inside me
Is a power only from love
That your fingertips have set free

Before, it was all an image
An illusion not at all real
But please, no more foolishness
It's love; love, that I feel.

Alone
Leave me alone
And let me live
Let me find my share to give

I can only learn alone
From all I have to face
I can only find my home
In an undiscovered place

Let no one tread along my lines
For they may lead astray
Let no one's smile appear by my side
As I wake before the day

The world is huge as you have said
And there's room for many more
But why do you keep hiding away
From people bombarding my door

My head is warm from fever
My body aches from fatigue
My heart is sad from sorrow
And my mind is sick of intrigue

I need a clear blue sky to fall
And leave me with fresh air
I need a piece of land just big
For me to live my share

All you can give me is not a glance
And not a doubt or a question
You walk your way and I'll walk mine
I'll follow no one's suggestion

Leave me alone, and let me live
You've been no help, just hurt me
After all that's done, I'm left as one
So break this bind and free me.

Nothing is Real Anymore

Behind the wall
Is a cold, bitter shadow
I have built the wall
And taken it down
Seeing the shadow only made me frown

It laughed in my face
Made life a pitiful place
It grabbed my hand
Succeeding as it planned
I saw that dreadful grin
That told me I'd never win

So I built back the wall
And turned away
Not a tear would come
For they were all washed away

Nothing is real anymore
Behind the walls of minds
If you force yourself in
It's the shadow you'll find.

A Confession

Lord, I confess
Every now and then
I fall apart
I fall into the pit
The ugly pit of the devil

Every now and then
I break apart
I break apart my own ideas
And adopt those of others

Every now and then
I tear apart
I tear apart my faith
And commit my mind and body to sin

Every now and then
I fall apart
I fall apart from confusion
About my own confusion

Lord, I confess
Every now and then
I shed a tear for pain
Every now and then
I cry and complain

But please forgive
All I have done wrong
Please continue
To keep my soul strong

Please forgive
My temper and impulse
Please continue
My sincereness and honesty

I shall continue
As an angel of your kingdom
I shall cherish
My holy freedom.

This Day Will Be Good

This day will be good
'Cuz I've started with a smile
This day will teach me
All that is worthwhile

Of all the people I will see
Everyone will share my grin
'Cuz this day is starting good
Ever since I've lifted my chin

This morning is so wonderful
And I can make it last all day
Then all the people around me
Will feel the same way

When I leave that face in the mirror
To see all other faces in the street
You can be sure it'll be a wonderful day
For everyone I meet.

To Boy George

Oh, George, how you feel
Protected and so clever
Oh, George, how you be
Behind that mask forever

All that color you portray
It's all so lovely and sweet
But, George, do you feel like I do
When you step off the street

Behind those crystal blue eyes
Is there a trace of a tear
Underneath that outspoken dress
Is there a sense of fear

Oh, George, how you feel
Behind your world of pretend
It may be when you tell me
That your color scheme will end

It's fun to be protected
And amusing as well
But I can't feel the beat of your heart
And if you're happy, I can't tell

Oh, George, how you be
When you take off that pretty face.

Like a Rose Cut in Two

He's taken my rose
And left it out to dry
He's left me with the dried up crumbs
That were once red petals, so fine

He's taken my rose
Far away, the wind blew
He's left me confused and bare-handed
Like a rose cut in two.

To Dan

When you are there
I know the world is listening
Because I can say all I have to say
In those eyes that comfort me,
That respect me, and believe me
You give me that strong shoulder to lean on
Your ear listens to my sobs
Your smile dries up my tears
Then there's a feeling
Like I've been lifted from a grave
You've given me a chance
More than just forgiveness

There's a piece of my heart
That's been hurt by no one
And your warmth makes it beat
Stronger than Time, or Day, or a Dream
  could ever explain.

But what is the explanation
When we will all be gone tomorrow
What is the reason
When people kill and run away
All I ask is for a smile, a touch, a meaning
You make me smile, when I see your golden smile
You lift my soul, with that friendly touch
You give our friendship meaning
Which no explanation could give reason for

And when I have your friendship
Life and all its miserable attributes
Seem to fade away.

In This Big City

Here I am
In this big city
I know no one
And no one knows me

Here I am
Free to walk as far as I can
With my black case in hand
And my sights pointing forward

So many faces
Will they look twice?
So many sounds
Will they listen for a scream?

Here I am
In this big city
There's no more play

And life is new every second
In this big city
Here am I.

A Little White Dove

A little white dove
Came and picked me up one day
It carried me far
To where imaginations play

So soft were the feathers on its back
That I felt carefree
So blue were its little eyes
That my reflection I could see

My imagination began to stir
As the dove dropped me within a blink
I floated to the ground so soft
Where an angel gave me water to drink

Now, I'm not a dreamer, don't get me wrong
But this just came up suddenly
A little white dove
Flew down from above
And tapped my soul with love.

(untitled)

Just to hold you
in my arms
in my arms
Just to hold you
Just to hold you in my arms makes me crazy
makes me fine
makes me pretend that you are mine

Just to kiss you
in my arms
in my arms
Just to kiss you
Just to kiss you in my arms makes me fly
makes me spin
makes me hold on to a grin

Just to lose you
in a minute
in a minute
Just to lose you
Just to lose you in a minute breaks my heart
breaks my soul
breaks this pencil that I hold.

From the Steps

Such beauty does darkness possess
Even sitting alone
There's no fear about the air
Just a calm about the breeze

As the stars twinkle down at me
They create a magnificent peace
Like nothing else held me together before
Except this

There's no reflection in darkness
Like there is the shadow during day
And no one can see you crying
No one can see the grin on your face

When a hand reaches out to me
It isn't a question of whose it is
Because the darkness lets it warm me
Without feeling guilty

The night sounds keep me company
Telling stories of the dawn
When no one's up to see
How the stars fade away

But in darkness they will always appear
For the eyes who can see the beauty
And create the peace.

Understanding

It really is hard
I know you can't see
Because right now you don't feel
The same as me

I know I have to
I know I should
I have to get over you
I just wish I could

Thinking of being with you
Is such a nice thought
Then I come to reality
And see what it's brought.

You Turned Around

You turned around
And I saw your different face
It made me hurt
It made me cry
Because I thought to me
You'd never lie

Your smile was a frown
Your touch was cold
It made me angry
When you broke the hold

Insinuations you did make
When you had no place to say
You pushed me out this time for good
You've pushed my thoughts away

It made me hurt (like a knife in the heart)
And it made me cry (like rain falling down)
Because I thought for sure to me
You'd never lie.

(untitled)

When in the Fall
I feel a chill
You bring your warmth

When in the dark
I feel a fear
You bring your assurance

When in the present
I feel afar
You bring me back

With you around
It's so much easier
To deal with my mistakes.

Butterflies

Butterflies around me
Butterflies inside me
I can see all the colors on a butterfly
But I don't know what they mean

There's a red one flying around my arm
Does that stand for love?
There's another that is quite bizarre
Flapping in the tree above

Butterflies talking in my ear
What are they trying to say?
So many butterflies surrounding me
Lift me from this day.

There's a Girl I Know

There's a girl I know
She is so innocent
But she's hurting inside
She writes the most beautiful poetry
That she lets nobody read
She could never hurt anyone
But she's killing herself

Once upon a midnight clear
When the end of all my fears was near
I gave a smile and then a nod
But what a mistake had I laid before God

There's a girl I know
She hides behind trees
She peeks through curtains
To watch the parade
And when it's gone
She imitates the clowns

Once upon a midnight clear
When my mother's words I could not hear
I stood before a total stranger
No one warned me of the danger

There's a girl I know
She cannot cry
But a single tear
Runs from her eye
She kneels to the Lord
And prays with all might
To save her from
The world of fright

Red Rose Petals - Dana Djokic

So very young
And skin so fair
Who comes upon?
To bring such a scare?
So she hides behind bushes
And awaits the stranger
Ready to defend
From any ungodly danger

So prickly are the thorns
On a soft, lovely rose
Only to make her heart bleed
From everything she knows

But she keeps on writing poetry
To make the pain go away
She keeps on writing
Just to feel good for a day

There's a little baby girl I know
She's learning how to crawl
She only smiles and laughs
But has already been hurt by all.

To Nana

Don't leave me today
When I've finally escaped
Don't leave me this moment
When my life's been finally shaped

I'll hold you up Grandma
Just hold out for me
I'll pray for you Grandma
Just stay with me eternally

I live so far away
Yet I can still hear your heartbeat
I always listen for it
No matter what I am doing

You live so far away
But I still hear you saying
"For you I'll live forever"
"Just for you, I'll live forever"

So I've put the pieces together
Of the life you've built for me
Don't leave me now, I plead
Grandmother, don't leave me here alone.

A Girl I Know

There's a girl I know
(And it's not me)
She fights and fights
But she won't let herself be

I've tried to help her
I've tried to understand
But she kicks dirt in my face
She pushes away my hand

If no one can make her smile
Who is to blame?
If she won't bend slightly
Who can follow her game?

This girl I know
She is one and then another
It's so hard to follow
Because she's never one or the other

So I've kneeled, pled and cried to her
But she only keeps turning me away
If I can't help, then there is no help
All she can do is pray.

Depression

It's setting in
Now
I can feel it setting in
Once before
I was depressed no more
But now it's setting in

It's taking over
Now
I can feel it taking over
Once past
I thought it wouldn't last
But now it's taking over

It's winning me
Now
I can feel it winning me
Once in
It buries my grin
I know it's winning me

It's setting in
Now
I can feel it setting in
Once before
I thought I'd be depressed no more
But now it's setting in.

Depression (2)

Emptiness surpasses depression
Because with depression there is something
With emptiness there is nothing
Maybe not even hope

It's a hollow, hanging feeling
Like the lights should go off any minute
It's a quiet, waiting feeling
Like something called nothing should come

At least depression lifts itself
Emptiness just pulls down lower
With emptiness there is really nothing
Maybe not even hope

But wherever there is dark
There is one trace of light
Wherever there is garbage
There is one trace of beauty

Whenever there is no hope
There has to be hope
Because everything goes in circles
And what goes down (depression)
Must always come up (joy).

Ballerina

The quiet, poised ballerina –
Though she does not say a word –
Can tell you everything
You need to know.

Play for Me
(To Dad)

Play for me
That beauty you make
Play only for me
Of which love I can take

Blow your horn
'Til it rips out my heart
Play that shiny baby
'Til it trembles in every part

If you play for me
I will dance 'til dawn
Play that shiny baby for me
Until all my tears are gone.

The Flight of Life

Within a rainbow
Little angels dance
Through the flight of life
Appears a colorful romance

Surrounded by ribbons
A smile may spark
Within the flight of life
Feel color over dark.

Mr. Mime

Mr. Mime, I have a rose for you
You don't have to speak
Mr. Mime, this is a very special rose
It will help you when you're weak

Please hold it in your hands with care
I know you are very gentle
Please give it water every day
I know you are quite sentimental

Mr. Mime, with one little rose petal here
I will wipe that tear from your eye
I hope that rose will last forever
Because now I must say goodbye.

These Moods

These moods that carry me astray
Why do they take me so far away?
These moods that hinder my face
And leave my smile in another place
These moods that make my hands grow cold
Should someone very young feel so old?
These moods that scare off little bees
And make the cats hide in the trees
These moods that give me bumps on my skin
Why dost the evil spirit hide within?

So I pray, and pray
To remove the bad
The Lord does listen
Because he makes me glad

So I smile and smile
To rid of the bad
The Lord does listen
Because me makes me glad

But, oh, these moods he inflicts on me
Just to teach me a lesson
I've learned, learned and taught myself
That my own mood is the best impression.

On a Sunday Afternoon

Crawling the walls
On a Sunday afternoon
Even drives the cats crazy

Organize the files
Arrange the desk
Wipe the sink
Vacuum the carpet
Wash the towels

A tiny wind excites me
A soft patter invites me
Being bored is like. . .
Being out of your mind.

Sunday Afternoon

Just because I don't speak
Doesn't mean I'm not thinking of you
And on a Sunday afternoon
When even the cats are away
The emptiness pushes me
'Til I need to say. . .
I miss you!

Today

Today I see
A world that couldn't be freer
A world that couldn't be colder
A world that couldn't be happier

Today I see
My face that couldn't be sadder
That couldn't be wiser
That couldn't be happier

Today I saw
The rain as it came down on me
Rain that came from another place
Rain that doesn't exist in this world

Today I saw
But I have dreamt
And I still dream
And I will continue to dream
About the Happiness Beyond.

(untitled)

frustrates me
looks me down
but I smile
she only frowns

don't want to cry
tired of tears
trying to break away
from the lonely years

frustrates me
to psychotic ends
won't let me be
won't be friends

yet so simple
are the words we say
but the meanings she gives them
make me turn away

As the tears
run down my face
God paralyzes me
I'm trapped in another place

He hears -- listens
You talk -- mock me
Stop destroying
and please stop putting yourself ahead of this time,
because ordinary people like us can't keep trying to
catch up -- it makes us all weak when we have to
guess where you are and it makes us all crazy when
we have to match your words with your actions, so
please. . .stop. . . .stop. . . .destroying. . . .us.

The Happiness Beyond

So many times
I've reached for the Happiness Beyond
So many times
Has my hand been pushed away

So I continue to reach
For the Happiness Beyond
And I continue to hope
That I'll grab it some day

We stand in single file
Against a solid brick wall
And those who get the bullet
Hopelessly must fall

We stand in single file
Behind each other, awaiting the rope
But those who run to get away
At least have some kind of hope

Something doesn't want me to smile
Something laughs when I cry
Something awaits with a silver bullet
And to get me, will continue to try

But I stand in the single file
Against the solid brick wall
I dodge and dodge the shots
Because never will I fall

I continue to stand in single file
Behind others awaiting the rope
But once every while I run away
Because never will I give up hope

Not until I reach the Happiness Beyond.

You Used to Sing to Me

You used to talk to me
Now you only smile
You used to sing to me
Sing verses for a while

You used to walk with me
Through the glorious rain
You used to comfort me
And ease my pain

Now you never talk to me
And a single tear runs from my eye
You used to always sing to me
And wipe all my tears dry.

The Glorious Rain

Like kittens will cry
And scratch at the posts
Waiting for the rainbow
I am -- walking through
The glorious rain

The rain, rain
The glorious rain
Where my thoughts had left me long ago
The rain, rain
The glorious rain
Where I find the verses I should know

And watch the people all walk by
Not one will stop and bid me 'hi'
Not one will smile or wave a hand
They all keep walking to a deserted land

And like the weak become strong
Like the cowardly become brave
I walk among the clowns
Through the glorious rain.

Paisley

Her name was Paisley
And she didn't say a word
But the words in her mind
Were the words that were heard

All she did was smile to me
But she told me many things
Paisley -- why do you play games with me?
Mystery is all you bring

I watched her leave the busy square
Through a crowd that didn't see her
But then all at once, they turned around
For Paisley had left her picture.

The End

The end!
It's here!
There'll still be tears,
There'll still be fears,
But no more helpless,
lonely years!
No more!

This Life!

This life!
It tortures me so
Oh, how I wish to just sleep
And forget
Just forget. . . .
Everything.

So Red the Rose

So red the rose
Through a child's eyes
So do my eyes water
From endless lies

So velvety are the petals
So rough and calloused are my hands
Working and working
To carry out other's demands

Love does make us bleed
And love does make us cry
But so beautiful is the pain
When we know the reasons why

So honest is my smile
So warm is my touch
So red is the rose
That's why I love you so much.

Dear Friend

I was just thinking about you
And I thought of all you say
You always seem to comfort me
In my lowest and saddest days

Dear Friend I'm depressed no more
And I wonder how happy I can be
But as long as I have you, Dear Friend
Sadness, I will never see.

(untitled)

and what
does it all
come down
to?
Please don't
tell me
Please don't
warn me
Please don't
say it
for it will hurt
if I hear the words
if I feel them
in my ears
and what
does it all
come down to?
Please hide me
Please take me away
To a place
Where I can be alone
where I can hide
in my very own thoughts
where no distortions
will appear
where dark is light
and light is dark
and Heaven is Earth
and the Earth shall be Hell
but I can pretend
I can dream and pretend
that none of this is happening.

Slave

If I may be a slave
On this lonely, helpless Earth
Then all I ask
All that I will ever ask
Is that you smile
When you tell me what to do.
Thank you.

(untitled)

And anyone
Who can look me in the face
And tell me
I'm not what I am
Is only a coward
Learning to talk.

(untitled)

I appear to be flesh
But I'm a ghostly saint
I appear to be a mind
But I am only a child
. . .Only a child.

The Glorious Rain #2

The Glorious Rain
Has befallen upon me
Soaked
And drenched
Is my own mind and body
With my own knowledge and wisdom.

Alone (2)

My friends
Have all vanished away
In another year
Another loss

In another year
Another thought creeps by

But what was meant to be
Was established in the beginning
In this world
I am alone

In this world
I will always stand alone.

Juliet

Juliet,
Many roses do you pick
But does your Romeo ever come?
Never does he show

And even in the winter
When the petals freeze over
She waits for some sunshine
To melt the frost away

In the brisk evening air
While the snowflakes fall
Juliet waits for Romeo
But never does he call.

First Love

There was a first love
That was the only love
Which brought on many tears
Which brought pain through my years

There was a precious love
An only love
That brought on much distress
Such everlasting distress

It was that first and only love
That has always remained in my heart
Not any other love
Has so fiercely taken me apart

There was a very first emotion
An emotion of caring fear
There was a very first feeling
A feeling of having love so near

Still I hold on to that first love
For an eternity shall I keep it
With a million more tears
A million more sad and painful years.

So Sad Am I

So sad am I
That no longer can I cry
So hopeless
Are my thoughts
So dry
Is my smile

I reach out
And no one is there
I look in the mirror
Only to see a stare
I've tried to love
But my love withers away
I've tried with all hope
But not for long will love stay

So sad am I
That my eyes are seemingly dry
Not a single tear
Shall ever appear
For so sad am I.

The Glorious Rain #3

No more verse
Will ever break the curse
Befallen upon me
                        Only the Glorious Rain
                        Can wash it away.

Roxanne

Roxanne, Roxanne
What a terrible mess
Please try to clean it if you can

Roxanne, Roxanne
Where is your mind?
Please try to find it if you can.

Miserable Attributes

When nothing works
Let me dance
Just let me dance my heart out

When no one understands
Just let me dance
To slow, sweet melodies
Pop, snappy tunes
Symphonical classics

And life
And all its miserable attributes
Will soon fade away.

Spring's Hope

Outside it's cold
Because winter has no mercy
Winter traps all innocent
And freezes their souls
To brittle ice

Outside it's windy
Because winter fears no pain
It blows away senseless dreams
For the meek are only senseless

Bring on Spring!
For dear Winter is nasty
No mercy prevails
No comfort in its air

Bring on Spring for us innocent
And drown Winter in Spring's glory
In Spring's hope.

My Many Moods

Like an angry wave
Rushing in from the deep
Like thunder
Rolling down from the sky
Like sweetness
Of a summer day
Like peace
On a moon-lit night

My many moods
Would never lead me astray
Not as yet.

Behind Me is My Shadow

Behind me is my Father
Who has never seen my face
Yet continues to look me in the eye

Behind me is my shadow
That continues to follow me
Wherever I go
Seeing that I get my way
Because it believes
That I have earned it

Behind me is my principle
Set up for me
And directed for me
But my shadow stands before me
And changes that principle
To how I like it

When no one guides you
And no one believes you
Rely on your shadow
For it may be behind you
But it is always in the lead.

Kirstie

Kirstie does not exist
Just a name
But I liked it so
That I named this poem just that

Kirstie could be an angel
Or a little, little kitten
Maybe a baby pig
Or the face on my sister's mitten

Kirstie reminds me of the sky
Kirstie could be a tire swing
Kirstie shines as warm as the sun
Or is the glare on a diamond ring

Kirstie is long silky hair
Also poised and positioned ballerina's feet
Kirstie is an unknown
Someone you've always wanted to meet

But all in all, Kirstie does not exist
Just a name
But I liked it so
That I named this poem just that.

Letters

We write letters
You and I
I write ten pages
You write nine

We always say the same thing
Wondering when it will all end
But we continue to write letters
To each other as friends

I send you my heart
When we write letters.

A Noise

There's a noise
In this house
It doesn't stop
Because it knows I'm here
And continues to annoy me

This noise
Makes me want to get away
Clever plan.

Mind Games

Mind games
Have us all trapped
All running
Running around in circles we create

Mind games have destroyed
The peace,
Beauty
And tranquility of innocence

Who are we fooling?
Who wants to fool us?
Where can I find the honest one?

Oh, Honest One
Where hast thou fled?
Far away from my innocent soul

As we try reaching each other
We only get lost
In our own mind games
Mind games, so funny.

All in a Day's Thoughts

You were
All in a day's thoughts
Only your face
Appeared and appeared again

All today
Only one thing was on my mind
And that was you

Only you
Could possibly fill my day
Fill my hours
Fill my moods

Only you
Could make me write this much
Write this fast
And think of such

Only you
Were in my thoughts today
Only your face
Appeared and appeared again.

A Pounding

There's a pounding
When there's concentration

An incessant throbbing
That I can feel
In my heart

There's an overwhelming fear
An unexplainable energy
A devastating surge of reality

There's a pounding
That I can feel
In my heart
And one word can describe it. . .

Success.

Finish What You Start

When choosing
Between one or another
There's a blinding of wit
And my skill takes cover

Oh, help me
Help me decide--
For this is my future
This is my destiny. . .
We cry

Yet so simple and elementary
Are the games our minds play
An idea pulls here
A feeling pulls the other way

But take that feeling
And finely take it apart
You can clearly see your answer
And that is to finish what you start.

All Very Young to be Sad

Yellow paper
Makes me happy
And white makes me sad
So I only buy yellow

To think of brushy grass fields
And hills towering wide
Wakening little roses
That have merely nothing to hide

Smiley little babies
Fluffy bunnies
Raindrops beating
Grandma baking

None of it comes from white paper
...all from yellow

I think of crystal waters
Tall leafy trees
Scrambling squirrels
And flapping birds

An echo after midnight
A song before dawn
A grip of my friend's hand
Lets me know I'm not alone

Gleaming, glistening, glowing
We are all still very young now
All very young to be sad.

Valentine's Day

It's Valentine's Day
And I'm sitting here
Thinking of you
Wondering if you're thinking
The same as I

Can you hear my heartbeat,
Heartbeat, heartbeat
Can you hear my heartbeat
Because it pounds for you

I'm someone else's Valentine
And you're someone else's too
But do you wish that I be yours
As I wish for you?

Today is only one day
That will finish off quite fast
But a million days will follow
And I'll keep trying until the last

Until you are my Valentine
My one and only Valentine.

Time for the Sun to Shine

This foolish heart!
Shall deceive me no more!
For all that happiness stands for,
I can bear
For all that fulfillment stands for,
I can bear

I have proven to myself!
Once and for very all!
That sadness cannot overtake me!
And strength won't let me fall!

On this Glorious Earth
Have fallen many rains
But now it's time for the sun to shine!
Time for the sun to shine!

My Precious Moments

My precious moments
At this age so very young
I choose discreetly
And hide my thoughts

My precious moments
Bear visions of joy
Between two people

My precious moments
Bear feelings of content
Between two people

My precious moments
Are a perfect picture
And no darkness enters

No poison prevails
No death delivereth –

My precious moments
Are of my younger self
Untouched by reality
Very calm and undisturbed
Very rewarding to the mind,
And very pleasing to the soul

God giveth me these precious moments,
Because mankind taketh everything else away.

Silly Words

This is but a puzzle
Dear Reader, if you must know
But don't try to figure it out
Because I, myself, do not know
It's just a mass of words
Trying to explain a feeling
Just a page of silly words
With a silly meaning
But, oh well,
We move on . . .
Sometimes a silly word can say
All you've ever wanted to hear
Sometimes that silly word can also
Bring about a tear
But this whole book is full of them
Silly, silly words
That if people were to read them
They'd laugh, laugh, laugh
But I mustn't call myself a silly word
For I put this all together
No silly mind
No foolish heart
Could ever be so clever
And so,
We move on . . .
To figure out these silly words
Would only be a game
But games we always play
As silly as they are
Games we always play.

Princess, What are You Waiting For?
(To Millie)

Princess, what are you waiting for?
Prince Charming to come knock on your door?

Well, have you looked?
He is already there
If you were watching,
You'd be aware

Princess, Princess -- how you speak of love
But can you see it, coming from above?
The sweetest you will ever find
The best love of its kind!

It's from a friend, so very near
Whom you told your secrets, so very dear
And he's given you all he's ever had
Just to keep you from being sad

Princess, what are you waiting for?
When Prince Charming is already at your door
You know you want to invite him in
Because you must be together for either to win

Princess, Princess -- so easy is your reach
Love is waiting for you at your door
It's that one and only Prince
Who you've waited so long for.

Stirring of the Heart

What can cause
A stirring of the heart?
Does a peaceful glance
Invite subtle romance?

How will I know
If he's thinking of me?
Will my heart skip a beat?
Will I feel it inside me?

This stirring of the heart
Causes much stirring of my mind
Yet I always feel
That love I will never find

But I feel it now
And so powerful can it be
I often pray
For it to set me free

Because I don't want to hurt
And I don't like to cry
That's all I've done
And can't explain why

Why, does he do this to me?
Keeps leading me on
Keeps stirring my heart
Then dropping me down

It's such a strong emotion
So very hard to let go
'Cause this stirring of the heart
Is all I have to let me know. . .

That I'm in love.

Realistics

Bring me realistics
Not a television set
Bring me realistics
Not a punk in disguise

Bring me someone's heart
That's been torn as mine
And explain to me their fate
Since their blood doesn't shine

Don't give me cartoons
Or magazine beauties
Don't give me polished prints
Or plush tapestries

But show me the soldier
Who sheds a tear for home

Show me the sun rising
And the moon cracking
Or the rain pouring
Even kittens whimpering

Bring me realistics
So that I may understand
What this is all about

So that I may follow
These games people play.

So Be It

So
Be
It
If
You
Shall
Leave me.

So
Be
It
But
I
Shall
Never
Leave you.

He Always Has That Way

He always has that way
Of weakening me
Of blinding me
Uncovering my soul
To reveal my faithful traits
But as I gather my strength
And open my eyes
I see what he will not reveal
To me
That he is a liar
Scaring my true feelings away
He is but a crook
Stealing my happiness away
And he is but a fool
That has taken my heart
And given it back broken
Yet he always has that way
Of finding me
In my weakest moments
To pull me in his world
Of splendor and love
Of all true things womankind dreams of
But he always has that way
Of leaving me here
To defend myself
Of which I have become strong
So, so strong
To awaken from this silly dream
And take my heart back in one piece
Until he appears again.

You Are So Far

You are so far
That I must say your name
To feel that you are mine
But are you?

You are so far from me
That I have to look at your picture
To remember who you are
But who are you?

You are so very far
That at night I only dream
In the day I only have my thoughts
To tell me that you are mine
But are you really?
I don't know. . .
You are so far.

I've Given You Away

From many hours
In the span of life
How many are lost
Upon thinking of foolish things. . . .?

Many,
Oh very many
For children grow up so fast
And they yet don't understand

I've given you away
For I am much too young
To be figuring out your trivia,
Contemplating your strategies,
And accepting your grievances

I've given you away
Before you ruin me one more day
But I haven't given up
Oh no – I haven't given up anything.

That Perfect Feeling

That perfect feeling
Shall I come upon it one day?
Shall I know what to say?

Dance with me this evening
And try to move as quick
Keep up with this rhythm
Put forth a perfect step

As we know in ballet
Your mind moves with your body
How well you concentrate
Tells you how to move

Time will discipline
But hope will train us
To believe anything

And now I believe
I believe I will achieve
That perfect feeling.

Halloween

I choose to hide
So no one can figure
No one can suspect
No one can guess

I choose this costume
So others will laugh
Others will cry
Others will gossip

I choose to make believe
So that no one knows I'm here
No one can see my glassy eyes
And my family can't find me

Even as it isn't Halloween
When children wear those silly costumes
I choose to put my face
Behind this silly disguise

I choose to hide
I choose to sneak away
I choose to shelter my thoughts away.

(untitled)

So long as I have
This feeling

And so long as I have
My will

I shall remain
Oblivious to such petty things.

(untitled)

Why must I be faced
With such trauma
As if simple things
Do not matter . . .

Oh, How I Wish You Wouldn't Leave Me

Oh, how I wish
You wouldn't leave me
When you are the only one
Who knows my hurt
Who knows my pain
Who makes me feel
Like there's something to gain

Oh, how I wish
You'd never leave me
Because I'm all alone
Just by myself

Even though
Your heart is always with me
And mine is always with you
I still wish
Oh, how I wish
You wouldn't leave me

Missing

Like a summer's day
I remember when
I used to play
Play on my thoughts
Thoughts of being free

And now that I am free
I cry for my fear
I cry for what is missing

Like a soft, warm wind
I think of lonely nights at home
Which were not lonely at all
As compared to nights spent here
And all for this freedom

I remember when
I used to play
And ponder my thoughts for a day
And now that I am free
I need someone close to me

For everything is missing

(untitled)

Inasmuch as I am
What I care to possess;
And inasmuch as I feel
I am what I possess;

I have nothing.

This is the Year

This is the year
I will achieve fame
This is the year
I will end all these games
No sooner than the present
I will take into effect
No later than tomorrow
I shall rise; I expect

This is the year
Of the Glorious Rain
That will pour and pour
To wash away pain
This is the year
Of the strong and the weak
The childish and the foolish
The bold and the meek

This is the year
Of music and play
For rhymes to happen every day

This is the year
For me to succeed
To drop all this silliness
And take on the lead

And so beautiful are the roses
Planted in my grandmother's garden
They shall bloom again this year
This is the year for all glory.

Fairy Tale, Rare

Curtains blowing in the wind
Ribbons flowing from her hair
Such magic only exists
In a fairy tale, rare

The freshness on her face
The pretty pastel slippers she wears
Such eloquent magic only exists
In a fairy tale, rare

Birds are singing
The sun is smiling
Children are playing
Butterflies are flapping around
this summer day

'Tis only a fairy tale
Is what they say
But I do believe
It will come true one day
I do believe, indeed.

In the Quiet of it All

In the quiet of it all
There is really no fear
The darkness is lifted
And my thoughts are at ease

In the quiet of it all
My heart beats calmly
My breath is eased
And my spirit is new

In the quiet of it all
No speech is senseless
No rule is broken
And I may lay to rest
For that quiet time
Until the chaos starts again.

There is No Worry at All

There is no worry
There is no wonder
There is no pain
As big as a truck
As huge as this earth
As large as the universe

There is no deed
There is no gift
There is no prayer
As small as a pebble
As tiny as a pin
As little as my thumb

There is no worry
As big as all the worry
There is no worry
At all

Sit back and relax, my friend
Put your uneasiness behind you
For all the worry
That you worry
I'm telling you
There really is no worry at all.

For this Movement

For this movement
In my soul
I dream of you

For this stirring
Of my heart
I long for you

For this restless mind I have
I hope for you
To come some day
And make my worries go away

For this movement
That awakens me at night
I long to have you in my sight

And I dance because my heart
needs it
I dream because my mind
needs it
But I hope for my soul
just to have you.

Things

Oh, so long is this day
That I must stop and ponder
Upon wishful things
Out of my reach
So hard is it to concentrate
On other, meaningful things
But to waste my time
Upon such wishful things
Yet it is on these long days
That I constantly hope
For those dynamic things
I constantly dream
Of such precious things
And before I realize
The long day has gone
And drifted into another day
Which slowly leads to another
Until I have reached the end
And time has passed away
No more long, lonely days!
I lay down to rest
Thinking back on all those dreams
And how silly it was
To ponder on such thoughts
And find that my life
Has passed me by
Oh my, oh my
What have I gained?

It Rings a Bell

It rings a bell
That face you make,
Of all the love from me
You had to take

Yet I often wonder
How it would have been
With you and I
And this love we're in

I wish someone would just take me away
I'm tired of telling you
I want you to stay

It rings a bell
That face you make
Of the heart in me
You had to break

I wish someone would just take me away
Take me away; far, far away.

Play Me Violins

Play me violins
To make me sad

Play me violins
To see my smile

Play those violins for me
And I will dance 'til dawn
Play those precious violins
'Til my fear is gone

Throw roses at the bride
Flip a quarter in the sea
But find a classic violin
And play it all for me

Bejeweled

Shimmer on my shoulder
Glitter in my hair
Rhinestones on my fingers
And sparkles everywhere

Like diamonds they will glitter
And like kittens they will cry
My tears continually roll
And never seem to dry

Crystal baby raindrops
Rubies, oh, so fine
No one's teardrops shimmer
As incredibly as mine

A rainbow shines right through them
With swirls of flowing bliss
Sparkle me and shimmer me
Bejewel me with a kiss.

Rarities

These yearnings for color
For rarities
And delicacies,
I only wish for
To satisfy my mind
Yet, not my heart

My heart yearns
For those things
Which only you and I
Can create together

Yet rarities
Do not come easy;
So is true
Of this love I wish to portray
But love is a rarity
Only you and I
Can create together

I watch people
As they laugh
So much excitement and enthusiasm
In the air

I also see
Their hearts cry for love
As they are what makes
Love so rare

Before I Wave Goodbye

Before I wave goodbye
To you
I leave you with this
Before my final thought
Of you
I blow my last kiss

No one has ever taken my heart
And broken it like you
No one has ever entered my life
And left without telling the truth

So many starry nights have left me
Staring up in wonder
So many rainy days have passed
Where my heart has pounded like thunder

All those times I'd see your smile
I'd find it was only a dream
Never have I been deceived so much
By the flow of a lucky stream

Before I wave goodbye to you
I shed just one more tear
Before I try to forget about you
I abolish all my fear

Because no one has ever taken my heart
And broken it like you
No one has ever entered my life
And left without explaining the truth

I've hoped and prayed too much
For a dream that would never come alive
I never found my strength so exhausted
For something impossible, I wanted to strive

Red Rose Petals - Dana Djokic

Now I tear the roses from my party
I will lay them out to dry
The only remnants I will ever have
Of a love that was such a lie

My heart has bled a thousand times
No more shall I watch it ache
No more shall I look into your eyes
And make such a foolish mistake

I can probably go very far
And never choose to look back
But if I come upon you one day
I will choose another track

Such a love I thought was perfect
I now know never existed
You choose to share with someone else
Your love that I enlisted

I wish someone would just take me away
So I can never remember your smile
But it hurts so much to just forget
It hurts to set it aside

But before I wave goodbye to you,
I want you to know what you've done
You've put a knife in my heart
Like no one else has ever done

And I write this ballad just for you
For someone to sing one day
I write this pain so you can see
What makes me feel this way

Because no one has ever taken my heart
And broken it like you
No one has ever entered my life
And left without explaining the truth.

I Turn This Page

I turn this page
For you and me
So that we can both be free

I turn this page
For you and me
So my love you will never see

I turn this page
One final time
To start again this game

I turn and turn
'Til there is no more
No more, no more, no more.

A Letter

Instead of the usual letter
I thought I'd write this way
I thought I'd find something interesting
To brighten up your day

I'm stuck in this old place here
That I supposedly call home
No one comes to visit me
Except you -- when you're alone

Everyone is out having a good time
While I'm sitting here all sad
When nothing seems to go my way
I harden and become all mad

I know you understand my ways
You put up with me a great deal
I just wish that others, too
Could see the way I feel

I thought of how much I love this guy
And laughed at my own disgrace
I push so hard to make him see
But he won't look me in the face

My so-called friends are miles away
They only call to tell their sorrow
But I wonder if they'd come to my side
If anything should happen tomorrow

What kind of life is this?
For a blooming 18 year old?
Might as well just lock me away
Throw my heart into the cold

I tell you Dan, I just don't know
I've tried to figure it out
But just when everything is going good
Something starts a bout

How much longer will you and I
Have to fight for what we need?
I'm tired of hoping and praying all day
No more do I want to plead

Might as well put my hands down
But I hate to say, "I give up"
I hate to say I've exhausted my skills
-- out of all my luck

I continue to be your special friend
So you continue to be mine
I hope we make it through together
I hope we come out fine.

(untitled)

Just when I catch you
In that smile
Oh, I happen to miss it
It only stays for a while

Just when I catch you
In that sparkle of your eyes
Oh, I happen to miss it
Just a bunch of lies

Just when I catch you
When I touch you
When I have you

Oh, I happen to miss it.

For Only This Day

For this day
I feel exhausted
For only this day
I feel I've lost it

I sleep and sleep
To brighten and shine
I dance and dream
To keep feeling fine

Because for only this day
I shall bow my head down
But after my heart plays
No more shall I frown

And after I talk to you
I know I won't feel the same way
But for now I feel exhausted
Yet only for this day.

He Was Lying In the Grass

He was lying in the grass
Looking up at the sky
Asking why he let her go
Wondering why, oh why

He was lying in the grass
Thinking of what he'd said
Thinking he should have mentioned
That he loved her instead

No time to think about
What she's done
No time to figure out
Who actually won

He was lying in the grass
Dreaming of what he gave away
Hoping and praying, like I did
To get it back some day.

Let Me Go

Why don't you
Let me go
Let me be
Set me free

Break the hold
You've turned so cold
Just let me be
And set me free

No love in your eyes
No warmth in your heart
Why can't you see
It's tearing me apart

Let me go
Away from you
Or tell me why
You don't love me too

Get out of my mind
When your love I can't find
Why don't you just
Let me go
Let me be
Set me free.

No More Writing

No more writing.
It ails me so!
To write this such!
When no one will know
Why it means so much.

Goodbye,
And let me live
My own way
And let me die
For yet not another day.

I Feel You Breathing

You don't know my name
You can't even see my face
But something draws you near
Something tells you this is the place

You've been to Europe
Away for a long time
Now you've returned
And would like to be mine

I'll take your hand
And guide your eyes
I'll make you see
Past the cruelty and lies

Hold me while I shiver
At the thought of you turning away
But you say you'll never leave me
Reassure me that you'll stay

You still don't know my name
But I think about you
I know you hear me breathing
And I feel you breathing too.

Lamp Shades and Shells

Lamp shades and shells
Ribbons and crystal
Lined along my dresser
As though some sort of art
That's put in place of a dream
As though some type of balance
Between reality and insanity

What lies beyond darkness
No one cares to know
But I ponder and ponder
Never reaching a conclusion

Lamp shades and shells
Ribbons and Crystal
Laying around in a mess
As though a hurricane went by
Pretending to be a fantasy
But disguising a thief
Who wishes to take
My lamp shades and shells
My ribbons and crystal
My dried roses and porcelain
Away.

From a Lion's Den

From a lion's den
I ran and ran
Trying to escape
Saying "I know I can"

Running from shadows
Not even my own
Looking for a destiny
Resembling my home

From a lion's den
I fled
Came upon you
Instead

Thought I'd fall in your arms
What a much better place to be

We

Why is it that
I speak of we
When we have not yet
Even be

Why do I mention
You and I
When my, oh my
There's you, but not I

How come sunshine dawns on me
To make me think of only we
When we have not yet even be
No you and I
Just you, not me

Why is it that
I see just we
Nothing else, foreverly

Just you and I
Oh my, oh my
Just you and I
Some reason why.

O' By My Side

I cannot look so very far
Nor did I have to
'Cuz there you are

O' by my side
How we should be
Side by side
Just you and me

I cannot speak so very much
Nor do I have to
I just listen and such

O' by my side
Like it was meant to be
Side by side
Just you and me

I cannot cook
Nor can I sing
But if you look
True love I can bring

O' by my side
Please always stay
Side by side
We'll face every day

O' by my side
How we should be
Side by side
Just you and me

Mother Says I'm Crazy

Mother says I'm crazy
Sister tells me too
Know one thing for sure
The love I have for you

Daddy's run away
He won't care to hear
No one understands
Why I want you so near

You've got your own problems
Lord knows, I have some
But we can put all those aside
And wait for morning to come

You touched me, oh, so dearly
Melted my heart away
Now you're asking sincerely
That you want me to stay

Mother keeps accusing
Sister tells me too
But we know where it's better
So I'll run away with you

Elementary is this language
But can't you see it says so much
Why deal with big fat words
That only confuse you and such

Maybe I don't have to spell it
Because maybe you already know
But maybe, maybe, baby
You can feel what I'm trying to show

Mother, I'm not crazy
Sister, look at you
I'm just on a higher cloud
Floating in the blue

(untitled)

The most graceful art
is Love
So pure, so tender
So harmless, and timeless
It stays as long as the day
And beats farther into the night
Until the last soul alive
Gets a taste of it

When It Happens

Oh, it makes me wonder
When something happens
And it happens, oh it happens
To not only me, but also you
It happens, oh it happens
To us, not them, just us

When it happens, yes it happens
It makes me wonder
What happens to you, not to me
For it happens to both we
But you don't see
What it does to me
When you walk away
As though it never happened.

Somewhere in Everlasting Speed

Somewhere in everlasting speed
Where silence escapes our ears
There is a moment of peace
A moment of truth
And a moment of love

Yet when the world
Moves around us too fast
We miss seconds by the hour
Losing our own peace
Our truth
And love
To be left with nothing

Wealthy men have everything
Running around and flaunting
But I, alone, have nothing
Only my good, honest thinking.

Rise

Like a slow moon rising
We can all awake
From the depths of gravity
Which pull us to misery
Rise, rise, rise
And let the bliss of the sun
Free the mind
Lift the burden
Free the heart
That's been hurtin.

Home Free

Home free
Please take me in
Home free
Is where I want to begin

Under a roof
Sturdy and strong
Next to an arm
That couldn't do wrong

I look out my window
At the glorious view
Nothing for miles
And nothing to do

Home free
I'm finally in
Home free
Where do I begin?

The air is much finer
The trees are so tall
The morning is friendlier
When I hear the birds call

This is my place
To ponder and expand
This is the life
So easy and grand.

Leaving Town

Please don't tell anyone
I'm leaving town
Don't want to be mourned
Don't want no frowns

Tell not a soul
I'm moving away
They can make it without me
For many more days

I'm skipping this beat
For a nicer and better
Not gonna ring 'em
Or send 'em a letter

I'm ditchin' this ditch
Climbing to a new hill
Beggin' won't change me
I feel like this still

Please don't tell anyone
I'm leaving this place
They won't put up fightin'
They won't miss my face

'Cuz I'd like it that way
To sneak out with pride
The right way to do it
Without having to hide

No, this ain't hiding
It's leaving with peace
Settin' my soul free
Without givin' up the lease.

So Long Since I've Written

So long since I've written
To you this way
Do you welcome my tone?
Will you let me stay?

We've always been friends
Nothing has changed
The warmth still grows
But the ideas are rearranged

Ring out for joyous skies
In the name of Love
I still stand empty handed
No hope from above

Who will take me
For more than a day?
Who can hold me and love me
In your special way?

I won't ever give up
Because you've taught me so well
But neither will I decide
My soul to sell

Nothing is new
I'm just a little more quieter
Nothing has changed
I'm just a little more happier.

No More Pictures

No more pictures
Can you take of me
To pin up on your walls
Why is it my face you want to see?
When nothing else comes at all

With my face
You are in love
With my hair
You are infatuated
But you haven't gotten anywhere
You shouldn't have waited

No pictures
Should you take of me
No more memories should you keep
This bird has to fly away
On another branch my heart should lay

No sense talking anymore
I can't change your mind
Better search another place
For someone like your kind
I don't want to break your heart
Anymore.

Gray Monster

Seems like
Wherever I look
A gray monster hides
Waiting to grab me
From my peace
To tear me apart to shreds
And when I think I have a breath
It swallows me whole
And buries me in darkness
Where I can't even see my tears glisten
I only have to sit and listen
To the lesson that comes next
To the story I must lead
And to the truth I must prove
But why does everything
Have to be proven?
Why do answers not satisfy
questions anymore?
Who has to answer who anyway?
Seems like wherever I lay my hat
Someone steps on it
Or it flies away with the wind
Why do I lay it anyway?
So many things to think about
All by myself
That my face feels inside out
And outside in
And I feel like I'm talking to my inside
And no one can hear it outside.

The Big Day

Saturday's the Big Day
So I've heard
Over and over
Saturday's the Big Day
Who doesn't know?

And I have to be there
To watch my mother cry
I have to be there
To stand behind the bride

A bride indeed
A bride indeed
My sister all in white
And I have to be there
As it's her special night

Let me take it all in
First,
Sister,
Let me take it in
Before you run away from us
Before you walk away
Let us take it in, first
Before we send you on your way

Not even did you look behind
To fix your trailing train
We were all there, Sister
Standin' there in vain

Not even did you turn around
To bid a fair goodbye
And I had to be there
To watch my mother cry

I know this happens every time
One of us lets go
But never did you stop to see
Never did you know

And I have to be there
To watch my mother cry
I have to be there
To stand behind the bride

How much longer should I stand here, mother?
Tell me when I can leave
Don't want to spoil the fiesta
Don't want anyone to see me grieve

Saturday's the Big Day
So I've heard, I've heard, I've heard!
Stand behind the bride in white
And utter not a word.

No Such Agony

No such agony
Can compare to mine
Somewhere, somehow
Something got out of line

No such agony
Can measure up to this
How can I ever look at you
Or even promise you a kiss

No such agony
No such pain
That will stop this fury
Or end this rain

No such agony
Can ever wake me up
To realize this dream
That's shaken me up

It's rattled and rolled
'til it's throbbed in my head
This thinking of misery
And not mercy instead

What can I say to you
To make you see?
It's not true what they're saying
What's wrong is me

What can I say to you
To remove this mark?
You've left me standing
All alone in the dark

No such agony
Can compare to mine
Somewhere, somehow
Something got out of line

And you weren't there to stop me
Left me standin' all alone
You weren't there to teach me
I felt like everything was gone

No such agony
Can explain all the tears
That I will be crying
For these wasted years.

Goodbye

Goodbye
My once known soul
My beating heart
Goodbye my tearful eyes
My soft precious hands
Goodbye,
My golden locks
And some gray
My creamy shoulder
And listening ear
Goodbye my never known friend
You've taken the last part
That I have
You've taken the last breath
That I may breath
And even if I never again
Stand before you
I'll always love you
And always think of you.

This is What I Wanted

Although I sob
Alongside the edge of my bed
This is what I wanted
To me one day you said

Although I sit and read these verses
It doesn't seem to matter
This is what I wanted
For all my thoughts to scatter

Although I cling
To the bare edges of hope
You won't let me in again
Alone I have to cope

I know you'll walk on by
Only in the mirror I should stare
As this is what I wanted
And no more will you be there

Idiosyncrasies

This is all so funny
How come I'm not laughing
Who broke up the puzzle
And swept the pieces under a rug?
This is all so funny
How come I'm not laughing
I've pulled these puppet strings off
Yet I'm trained to move like this still
This is all so funny
You are there and I am here
I watch the same things all day
You play the same games all day
I never dreamt about this conclusion
So suddenly did things turn
I'm hoping it's only an illusion
But these idiosyncrasies keep coming around still.

After Mistake No. 3

Even after Mistake No. 3
Something else keeps following me
Something else keeps lurking beside
Not letting me escape
Not letting me hide

Even after Mistake No. 3
Some other evil keeps pulling me
I am God's child and always will remain
From these foolish antics
I shall refrain

Oh, Jesus
How could this be?
What have I done
for this misery to see?

Oh, Jesus
Where was the break
That caused me to initiate
This bloody third mistake?

Is there life
After Mistake No. 3?
I'll keep praying
And then I will see

Is there hope and understanding
After Mistake No. 3?
Or do I have to sit here and wait
Dreading my destiny?

Work Desk

All of a sudden I'm sad
Staring here at my
Big white work desk
How awkwardly I sit behind it
How bare it looks all the time

All of a sudden I'm sad
And looking out the window
Doesn't change things
Contemplating strategies doesn't rearrange things
Hoping and moping doesn't change things

All of a sudden I'm mad
Because I'm left all alone
After all I've done
I'm left all alone

I'll never ask for a thank you
But only one thing I'd like to see
Mother, Father, Sisters
Will you remember me?

All of a sudden I'm sad -
Waiting for things to get better.

Oh, How I wish it was April

Oh, how I wish it was April
So the sun can shine on my face
Oh, how I wish it was May
So I can run through rolling meadows

I can see Winter coming
Soon my windows will be frosted
My step rails will be iron cold
But I feel warmth in your heart
And that makes me think of April

Oh, how I wish it were dawn
So I can hear the birds chirping
Oh, how I wish it were dusk
So I can hear the owls hooting

And I loved to watch the moon
As it slid across the country sky
As I sat by my old dog
Remembering when he and I were young

Suddenly I have to pull a scarf
Over my face or it'll turn deep red
I have to hide my precious fingers
But I'd rather slip them into your hand instead

I can see the leaves rustling
All about with no place to go
And I wish I could be one of them
Just to fly and find my home

They tell me Winter's coming
And they're scurrying 'round about
Because they, too, are looking
For a place that's nice and warm

Red Rose Petals - Dana Djokic

Oh, how I wish it was April
When my mother made cookies in our basement
And my father put up the tire on the tree
I was the first on it, wee!

Oh, how I wish it was April
Once again, when flowers smiled at me
Soon I'll have that feeling again
But only after Winter's glee.

This Fragile Stem

In my hand I hold this,
This fragile stem
That I've picked

On the end it carries
A heavy load
A pretty rose's head

In my dainty hand I hold
This, this skinny pose
But after all I lay it down
Lay it down
So as not to break it.

Everywhere and Every Time

Everywhere I look
Your face appears
Everywhere I go
Images of you seem clear

Every minute of the day
I wonder where you are
Every second that you're gone
I wish you wouldn't be so far

Embrace me, my darling
Only then will I feel fine
Talk to me and sing to me
Only then will I know you're mine

Every time I hang up the phone
I long to call again
To hear your voice every minute
Is what I want, my friend

Every time I say my prayers
I dwell the most on you
I wonder if I'm in your thoughts
And in your prayers too.

I Wait

I wait
Like I wait for the train
I wait for the passing of pain
For the rising of good
And destruction of bad

I wait
For you to let go
For my instincts to tell me so
I wait like I wait for the train
For the passing of such pain

I wait
For the mailman to deliver
The garbage man to take away
For the officer to issue
For the manager to order
For the warden to lock

I wait
For the plane to land
For the car to park
For the door to open
For the light to turn on
For the agent to discover
For the nurse to inject
For the doctor to prescribe
For the coroner to pronounce

I wait
For the program to finish
For the alarm to go off
For the pot to boil
For the timer to ring
For the scale to break
For the polish to smear

I wait like I wait for the train
Ticket in hand, black case
Where is this train going anyway,
Mr. Conductor?
Even you don't know
So, why do you make me pay?
Why do you make me pay?

So Hard

This is so hard
So hard to swallow
This is so hard
My life's so hollow

This is so hard
So hard to perceive
This is so hard
What you want me to retrieve

This is so hard
So hard to contemplate
This is so hard
When you force me to relate

I look at two pictures
I can't decipher which is best
I think about you and others
But I can't give up the rest

I have it colored in my mind
What it is I'm looking to find
But this is so, so very hard
Nothing else is so very hard

Although you leave me roses
And you try to take my hand
It is so hard to let go
To feel this love so grand

I see it here before me
And still, a fool, I let it be
But when will I get what I'm looking for
Instead of just what I see?

This is so hard, my friend
So hard to swallow
This is so hard, and then
It leaves my life so hollow

This is hard, but yet
On other days it's easy
You make it so hard for me
Yet you always seem to please me.

Mama

Mama - here I am
Flagging you down
Do you see me?
Do you hear me?
Do you need me now?

Mama - I haven't seen you
In quite a long while
Do you hear me?
Do you love me?
I can see your smile

No one's hand is warmer than yours
No one's embrace is more genuine
No one's smile is bigger than yours
No one's heart is more understanding

Mama I am mistaken
To cry like this for me
But all my life I've shed these tears
And have cried to make you see

Mama I have been corrected
With this idea I have acquired
For of your love and always your honor
I shall never grow tired.

In This Dream: Reality

In this dream: reality
I'm standing in a lonely subway
Chewing my gum and reading a book
But even once, when I look
It doesn't seem real

In this dream: reality
I'm covered in my bed up to my ears
I stare at the closet and
Bring out all my fears

In this dream: reality
I talk to you and talk to you
But you don't hear the words
That I so desperately utter
So it doesn't seem real

In this dream
I fight and fight
I kill and steal and
Search for what is real

In this dream
I work and work and rest
Hoping, clawing, climbing
To one day be the best

In this dream
I run and sweat and run
Looking for a bit of laughter
Out of an ordinary fun

In this dream
I put on these clothes
I color them and make them
But hardly anyone knows

In this dream
I'm born and I die
I listen and learn
I scream and cry

I look it up in the dictionary
I ask people I don't know
But they can't explain reality
As it seems to be so

In this reality: dream
I write and pray
I meditate to moaning
And I decide to stay

In this reality: dream
I smile and I wink
I ride the train for hours
I play with my hair and think

In this reality: dream
I step inside
I suffocate to death
But I don't swallow my pride

In this reality
I wonder and wonder
About the aching of pain
And the sound of thunder

When skin doesn't feel so warm anymore
What does a cold white floor feel like?

When eyes stab a beating heart
How does a steel blade feel like?

When fingertips once felt kind
What do claws project to the mind?

In this reality that feels like a dream
Funny how unreal it all seems

Yet even now, as we have all become blind
One trace of Truth is what I will find.

Sadness of This Day

Sadness of this day
Shall not overtake
All I've built up
And filled up
And colored and painted
And cut and sewn
And sketched and drawn;
It cannot confuse
The white with the black
The top with the bottom
The front or the back;
It cannot juggle up
This everlasting struggle up
Or mingle and mix
My colored locking sticks;
It wouldn't crush or break
This glass of a mistake
It couldn't mislead or leave
When no longer will I bereave;
It's the 18th day
And the 9th of the year
No more shall I wake up
To face any fear;
I can grow my hair long
And put no color on my face
'Cuz Big Daddy this is it
Aint no better place;
And once more if I see it
I'll crumble it like paper
Throw it in the trash
Once more if I see it
I'll blind it with the whites of my teeth
Stab it with the blades of my eyes
Claw it with the tips of my fingers;
But the sadness of this day
Or any other day
Shall not overtake

All I've built up
And filled up
Acquired and saved
Fought for and wept for
Desired and craved.

This Tension

This tension is mounting
That surrounds us so
But somehow, never
I realize, you don't know

Either you don't know
Or you just don't care
Whatever the reason
You're never there

This tension is mounting
Around the halos on our heads
But I won't take mine off
Just to take you to bed

Either you don't know
Or you just don't care
Whatever the reason
It seems you're never there

I smell the winter coming
Soon frost will freeze my heart
But yours seems already frozen
Mine you've only taken apart

As each windy day passes me
I long to have you by my side
But somehow, never do you show me
Those feelings you choose to hide

This tension is mounting
That surrounds us so
But somehow, never
I realize, you don't care to know

Either you don't know
Or you just don't care
Whatever the reason
You'll never be there.

To Baby

You are my broadway
You are my sunset
You're my final destiny
The answer to my plea

You are my heartbeat
You are my sunshine, every day
You are my beauty
That will never fade away

Oh, Baby, how I love you
Because you're all I've ever wanted
Oh, Baby, how I'll keep you
In this happiness you've started.

To Mother

The decline of youth,
of innocence, and of happiness
is pain
in every way possible
pain in the hands
pain in the legs
pain in the back;
but the worst pain,
is the pain in the mind
creating all the other pains.

The decline of Mother,
even the word is fragile,
delicate and tender,
that one should know
to caress her gently
to speak to her softly
to think of her graciously.

Her trembling is from fear;
her tears are from pain;
but whatever the reason -
everyone is to blame.

Second By Second

The clock ticks
Otherwise it's silent
Second by second
It passes me by
As I sit here
And write
Not of love
Not of pride
But of just those seconds
That pass me by
That haunt my mind
Push me to edges
Leave me clinging
Pressing on my toes
To save precious seconds
Before they pass me by
And I wonder
How many
How many
How many more seconds
Before total silence.

Hi

Just a short note
To bid you "hi"
For never do I intend
To say goodbye

By your side
I'll always be
No one can stop us
Not you and me

We'll travel the world
And find our place
I know you can read
What's on my face

That's why I send this note
To bid you "hi"
For never do I intend
To say goodbye.

Sometimes Do I Let Them Get Away

Feelings.
Every so often
They appear
Pulling me to edges
It's very clear

Never have I seen you
In this way
Feelings keep on telling me
I want you to stay

Please let me feel your hand
Just one more time
Don't slip away
Without your love I'm blind

Feelings.
Sometimes when I'd never leave you
I'd play on those thoughts all day

Feelings.
When they start to pull my heart
Sometimes do I let them get away.

If I Could Write a Poem For You

Oh, if I could write a poem for you
It would be filled with enthusiasm,
Happiness and adventure
Oh, if I could just think of a few lines
To write in this poem
They'd be singing with sunshine
Rhyming with rhythm
Blazing with beauty
If I could put together a verse or two
It would be as long as a road
Stretching up to glowing hills
It would branch out like the fine limbs of a tree
And flower into silky, shiny leaves
That flutter as the wind sneaks by
And drip with dew in the morning frost
If I could put together just a few words
That could light up your darkness
Dance for your feet
And sing for your soul
If I could write just one poem for you
I'd burn all other poems I own
I'd write it in calligraphic romance
On paper as pastel as your cheeks
I'd write it just to see
The brightness in your eyes
And just to feel
The softness of your touch.

Worries

They don't see
What worries me so
I try to find it
But even I don't know

Nothing is ever easy
There's always a price to pay
With sincere manipulation
Things still don't go my way

Frost
And cold
Won't get to me
This warm heart
Will keep me free

Wind
And rain
Won't get to me
These strong hands
Will set me free

What worries me so
Oh, will I ever know?
Maybe it's nothing.

You Question Me So

Oh, raise me
But don't daze me
For I drift high when you're near
You question me so
Why, I don't know
No other heartbeat do I hear

Oh, place me
But don't erase me
For I am color for your slate
You question me so
Why, I don't know
But for you I'm never late

Oh, take me
But don't break me
For I am the post for you to lean
Why question me so
When anywhere I'd go
Just with you to be seen

You question me so
Why, I don't know
Nor do I answer
Nor do I
But curiosity do I show.

Blue Moon

Blue moon
In the midnight sky
You wait for me
To come home
You watch for me
To come walkin' up the drive
You light the way
And guide me in
For it's so late
And I should be sleepin'
But I been out with the owls
Prancing with the deer
Gawking with the hawks
Oh, blue moon
I just wish
In one starry night
When the path is clear
You could guide me home
Guide me home.

Why?

My heart aches
Why?
My blood freezes
Why?
My mind drifts
Why?

Touch you with cold hands
Kiss you with dry lips
Look at you with watery eyes
Speak with cracked phrases
Laugh with silent joy
Walk with forbidden pride
Dance with hidden sweat
Sing with trapped harmony

Who knows?
Why?
Why? Tell me.
Why?
Why know?
Why ask?

In the Company of a Bore (2)

Talk to me
Like lovers do
Oh, hush!
I won't say another word
But it's my heart, darling
That you've heard

You cannot speak
Or is it me?
That makes you turn
So foolishly

You gaze away
Please look my way
I won't say another word
But it's my heart, darling
That you've heard

Talk to me!
Don't look away
Don't be afraid
To tell me to stay

Oh, hush!
I shall speak no more
To find myself
In the company of a bore!

A Record

To record this
would be history
indeed
To write it down
would make news
To have it on paper
on screen
in memory
would cause a stir
indeed
So it's down
on lines forever
once in a lifetime
may never happen again

This dream
That I have to dream
This heartbeat
That I must control
This feeling
Exploding at all angles
Shooting out like stars
And glowing brighter than crystal
And here it is
Blue on white
Not in Chinese
Not in Russian.

We Don't Need Paper Flowers

We don't need paper flowers
To decorate the walls
We don't need satin dresses
To cover up the girls

Why do we need diamonds
Or ribbons to put in my hair
Why do we need Hallmark cards
To tell us that we care?

No thank you for your pastries
Please take back your cookie tray
Whatever it is that others need
We're still in love either way

Don't buy a new mattress
This old one's just fine
I'll rub your sore back
And you'll rub mine

Don't take me to Chicago
No difference does distance make
Whatever you lay beside me
It's you I'd rather take.

Through

Plastic face
Take it away!
From my fragile one

Imitated sorrow
Exaggerated joy
Take it away!

No more games,
Baby,
No more games!

Take your plastic mind away
I care not to talk to a wasted prey
Take your antics elsewhere son
If it's a fool you want – I'm not the one

Through!
All through!
With riots and rigs
With laughter and lies
And sheep and pigs
Take them away
And make them into glue
Take 'em away
With meaningless traps, I'm through!

We Sit And Watch The Symphony

We sit and watch
the symphony
as these two in front of us
hold hands and stare –
I wonder what is there.
They speak every minute
exchanging thoughts –
never do they look my way

We sit and watch
the symphony
never does he look my way
never does a word he say –
Just holds my hand
to keep the warmth
and glances over
to see me sitting here

We sit and watch
the symphony –
never does he bother me
but I hear him breathing
and he hears me too –
no words we speak
when such silence is true.

When I hear him
and he hears me –
we sit and watch
the symphony.

To Ring Your Doorbell

To ring your doorbell
Would seem off-key;
Would you have been hoping
That it would be me?

To knock on your window
Would be off-track;
If you didn't answer
Would you wish I'd come back?

To sneak through the porch
Would be such a scheme;
Would you throw me out
Or finish your dream?

Oh, tell me to stay!
We'll talk and have tea;
Stare out the window
Pretty flowers to see

Wake me, wake me!
I've missed my train
Alright, I'll stay
For there's something to gain

Never would I have rang it
If I thought it seemed off-key
Never would you have opened
If it was someone other than me.

The End (2)

I just wanted to add this
As sort of an ending scene
I wanted to put this in
So everyone will know what I mean

Thank you for this art, God
That others have brought out
If it wasn't for snobs and bums and jerks
This never would have come about

Thank you for this talent, God
That bitches and witches created
Because of them and their snickering
My art has made me elated

I could name a thousand names
To dedicate this to
But instead I just present this gift
Which will free me of my dues.

Alphabetical Listing

1. 1-2-3 35
2. 1980s' Design 2
3. A Confession 170
4. A Garden Full of Roses 93
5. A Gift of Gold 124
6. A Girl I Know 187
7. A Letter 261
8. A Little White Dove 177
9. A Moment 126
10. A Noise 224
11. A Picnic For Two 43
12. A Plea 163
13. A Pounding 227
14. A Record 320
15. A Rose Knows 82
16. A Shake 71
17. A Silent Song 132
18. A Stab 68
19. After Mistake No. 3 291
20. All in a Day's Thoughts 226
21. All Very Young to be Sad 229
22. Alone 168
23. Alone (2) 212
24. Along The Blazing Trail 83
25. Always and Always 117
26. And Anyone 209
27. And What 207
28. Another Way 78
29. Ask 134
30. At Such a Loss 160
31. Ballerina 190
32. Before I Wave Goodbye 258
33. Behind Me is My Shadow 221
34. Being Young 145
35. Bejeweled 256

36.	Blue Moon	317
37.	Born	135
38.	Butterflies	183
39.	By The Way	143
40.	Calm	47
41.	Candlelight	45
42.	Carry Me Through The Garden	159
43.	Cascades	20
44.	Change	120
45.	Color Me Red	46
46.	Dance	33
47.	Dear Friend	206
48.	Depression	188
49.	Depression (2)	189
50.	Drama	137
51.	Ears	110
52.	Everywhere and Every Time	296
53.	Expressions	129
54.	Fairy Tale, Rare	249
55.	Fatal Attraction	22
56.	Fear	99
57.	Finish What You Start	228
58.	Fire	76
59.	First Love	214
60.	Flip; Flippy; Flippant	38
61.	Foolish Distress	131
62.	For All it Seems to Be	136
63.	For Me	97
64.	For Only This Day	264
65.	For The Last Time	41
66.	For This Movement	252
67.	For You, Grandma	101
68.	Free to Dream	27
69.	From a Lion's Den	270
70.	From a Picture	127

71.	From Brother to Brother	31
72.	From The Moment	114
73.	From The Steps	179
74.	Frustrates Me	198
75.	Get To You	79
76.	God Forbids Me	148
77.	Goodbye	288
78.	Gray Monster	283
79.	Halloween	242
80.	He Always Has That Way	238
81.	He Was Lying in the Grass	265
82.	He Was Never Really Here	39
83.	He Will Yell	28
84.	Heaters	66
85.	Help	53
86.	Here's a Dime	30
87.	He's The One I Love	8
88.	Hi	312
89.	Home Free	279
90.	How The Kitchen Rug Lays	122
91.	I Appear to be Flesh	210
92.	I Feel You Breathing	268
93.	I Haven't Even Begun	106
94.	I Know We've Only Met	153
95.	I Turn This Page	260
96.	I Wait	297
97.	Ice	64
98.	Icecream	48
99.	Ideas	65
100.	Idiosyncrasies	290
101.	If Anyone Asks	6
102.	If I Could Write a Poem For You	314
103.	If I Write	104
104.	If Someone Would Sing	128
105.	If You Don't Approve	12

106.	I'm Here	36
107.	I've Given You Away	240
108.	In My Sleep	62
109.	In Place of Face	115
110.	In The Company of a Bore	140
111.	In The Company of a Bore (2)	319
112.	In The Quiet of it All	250
113.	In This Big City	176
114.	In This Dream: Reality	302
115.	Inasmuch as I am	247
116.	Inner Confusion	164
117.	Interest	77
118.	It Rings a Bell	254
119.	It's You	37
120.	Juliet	213
121.	Just to Hold You	178
122.	Just When I Catch You	263
123.	Kirstie	222
124.	Lamp Shades and Shells	269
125.	Laughing Up the Stairs	91
126.	Leaving Town	280
127.	Let Me Go	266
128.	Let Myself Sing	98
129.	Let's Talk Brother	44
130.	Let's Thank God	84
131.	Letters	223
132.	Life Rope	72
133.	Like a Rose Cut in Two	174
134.	Little Black Slippers	96
135.	Love, So Free	116
136.	Mama	301
137.	Many Starry Nights	167
138.	Maturity	150
139.	Mimi	102
140.	Mind Games	225

141.	Mira's Play	90
142.	Miserable Attributes	218
143.	Missing	246
144.	Moonlight	34
145.	Mother Says I'm Crazy	273
146.	Mr. B	146
147.	Mr. Right	103
148.	Mr. Mime	193
149.	My Hand	151
150.	My Many Moods	220
151.	My Precious Moments	232
152.	My Room	119
153.	My Style	3
154.	Never	73
155.	No More Pictures	282
156.	No More Writing	267
157.	No Such Agony	286
158.	No Such Word	161
159.	No Trace	55
160.	Nothing is Real Anymore	169
161.	Now What?	142
162.	O' By My Side	272
163.	Ode - On a Raindrop that Resembles a Tear	157
164.	Oh, How I Wish it Was April	293
165.	Oh, How I Wish You Wouldn't Leave Me	245
166.	On a Hill	112
167.	On a Sunday Afternoon	195
168.	On Pink Paper	125
169.	Once	123
170.	One	49
171.	One Day Will Be Mine	17
172.	One Man	108
173.	One Light	50
174.	Optimism	158
175.	Our Barn	109

176.	Out of One	152
177.	Paisley	202
178.	Paradise	139
179.	Passion	162
180.	Pink	63
181.	Play for Me	191
182.	Play Me Violins	255
183.	Princess, What are You Waiting For?	234
184.	Prison	70
185.	Rain	94
186.	Rarities	257
187.	Rays	42
188.	Realistics	236
189.	Reality	51
190.	Recurring Dream	165
191.	Rise	278
192.	Roxanne	217
193.	Ruby-Red Nails	111
194.	Run Again	100
195.	Sadness of This Day	305
196.	Second By Second	311
197.	Sensations	60
198.	Shout	32
199.	Signals	156
200.	Silly Words	233
201.	Sing	26
202.	Slave	208
203.	So Be It	237
204.	So Hard	299
205.	So Long as I Have	243
206.	So Long Since I've Written	281
207.	So Red the Rose	205
208.	So Sad Am I	215
209.	So Soon	130
210.	Some Day Soon	25

211.	Something, Anything	105
212.	Sometimes Do I Let Them Get Away	313
213.	Somewhere in Everlasting Speed	277
214.	Spring is Me	144
215.	Spring's Hope	219
216.	Still I Wonder	121
217.	Stirring of the Heart	235
218.	Suddenly	18
219.	Sunday Afternoon	196
220.	Talk; Just Talk	4
221.	Tell Me	21
222.	Tell Me (2)	23
223.	Thank You	19
224.	That Perfect Feeling	241
225.	That Picture	87
226.	That Piercing Sound of Anger	59
227.	The Big Day	284
228.	The Borderline	147
229.	The Brightest Star	89
230.	The Cold	86
231.	The End	203
232.	The End (2)	325
233.	The Flight of Life	192
234.	The Glorious Rain	201
235.	The Glorious Rain #2	211
236.	The Glorious Rain #3	216
237.	The Happening	107
238.	The Happiness Beyond	199
239.	The Light of Day	118
240.	The Maiden	80
241.	The Maple Tree	85
242.	The Meaning	29
243.	The Most Graceful Art	275
244.	The Night	154
245.	The Rhythm	14

246.	The Small Part	61
247.	The Stage	133
248.	The Stray Cats	40
249.	The Subtle Dance	69
250.	The Sun	75
251.	The Tree	58
252.	There is No Worry at All	251
253.	There's a Girl I Know	184
254.	These Moods	194
255.	They'll Always Be The Same	9
256.	Things	253
257.	Thinking About You	57
258.	This Day Will Be Good	172
259.	This Fragile Stem	295
260.	This is the Year	248
261.	This is What I Wanted	289
262.	This Life!	204
263.	This Reminds Me	13
264.	This Tension	307
265.	This Time	15
266.	Through	322
267.	Time	7
268.	Time for the Sun to Shine	231
269.	To Baby	309
270.	To Boy George	173
271.	To Dan	175
272.	To Mother	310
273.	To Nana	186
274.	To Plant A Garden	24
275.	To Ring Your Doorbell	324
276.	To The Brightest Eyes	95
277.	To Write A Poem	1
278.	Today	197
279.	Two Feet Away	88
280.	Understanding	180

281.	Valentine's Day	230
282.	Warm	56
283.	Wave Goodbye	67
284.	We	271
285.	We Are	54
286.	We Don't Need Paper Flowers	321
287.	We Sit And Watch The Symphony	323
288.	What a Fine Time	149
289.	When in the Fall	182
290.	When It Happens	276
291.	When It Rains	113
292.	When It Rains, I Think Of You	11
293.	When Lightning Strikes	16
294.	When The Color Changes	10
295.	When She Yells	141
296.	Who?	155
297.	Why?	318
298.	Why Must I be Faced	244
299.	Winning	92
300.	Work Desk	292
301.	Worries	315
302.	Wrapped Around a White Silk Sheet	74
303.	Wrinkles	52
304.	Wrinkles (2)	81
305.	You Are So Far	239
306.	You Question Me So	316
307.	You Turned Around	181
308.	You Used to Sing to Me	200
309.	You're Just a Punk	5

Red Rose Petals - Dana Djokic

Red Rose Petals - Dana Djokic

www.ingramcontent.com/pod-product-compliance
Lightning Source LLC
Chambersburg PA
CBHW031614160426
43196CB00006B/130